LEARN HOW TO DRAW
PEOPLE
FOR BEGINNERS

80 PRACTICAL exercises

Index

My name is:

· ·

Ready to draw! I'll teach you how with exercises you can do right in this book. **You just need a pencil.** Draw gently so you can erase and correct mistakes easily. **Let's get started!**

Draw these figures several times

Continue these lines to the end of the page

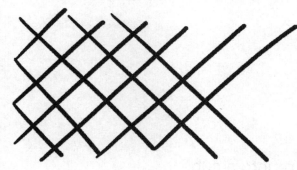

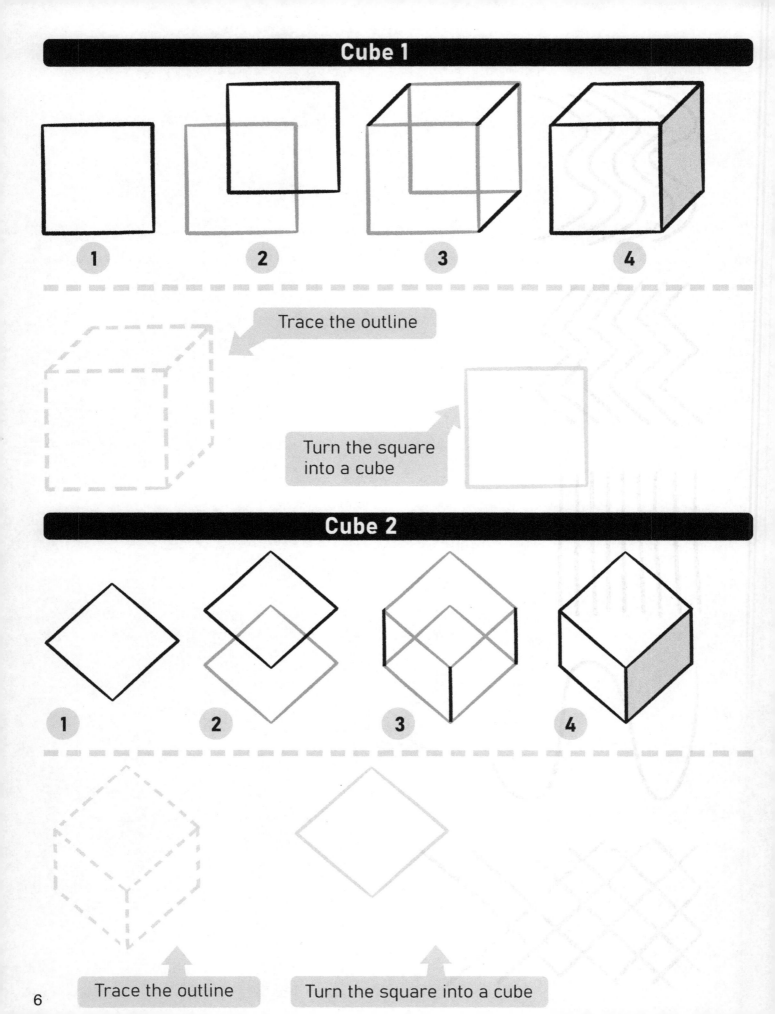

Cube 1

1 **2** **3** **4**

Trace the outline

Turn the square into a cube

Cube 2

1 **2** **3** **4**

Trace the outline

Turn the square into a cube

6

Cylinder

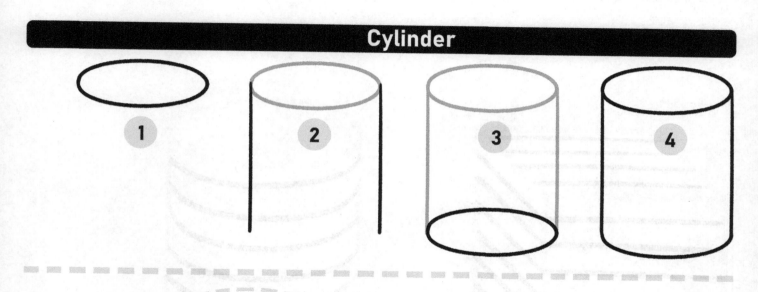

1 2 3 4

Trace the outline

Turns the oval into a cylinder.

Piramide

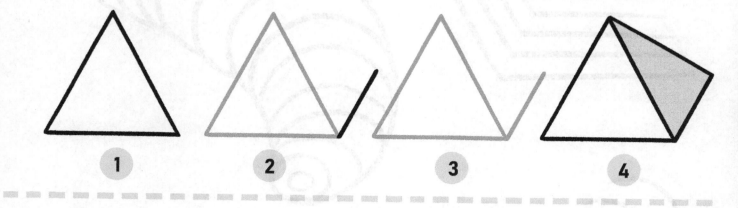

1 2 3 4

Trace the outline

Turn the triangle into a pyramid

7

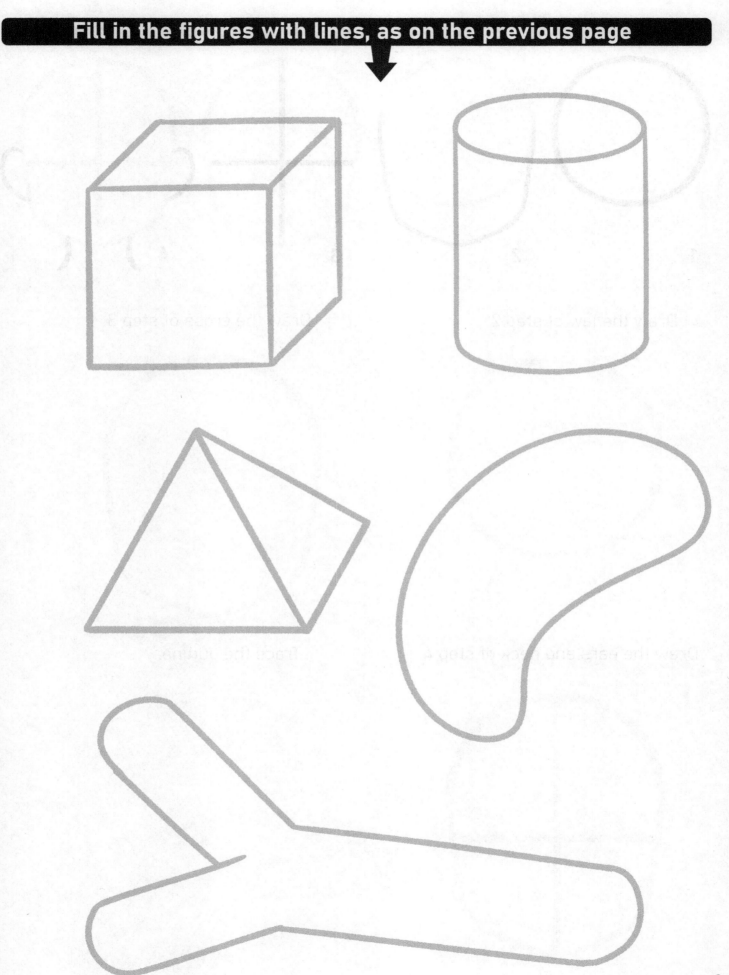

Step-by-step front view of a head

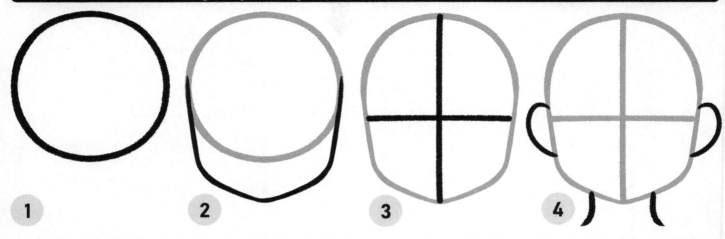

1   2   3   4

Draw the jaw of step 2

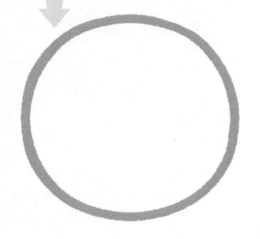

Draw the cross of step 3

Draw the ears and neck of step 4

Trace the outline.

Step-by-step profile view of a head

Draw step 2

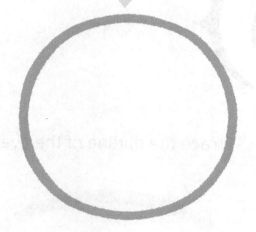

Draw the ear and neck of step 4

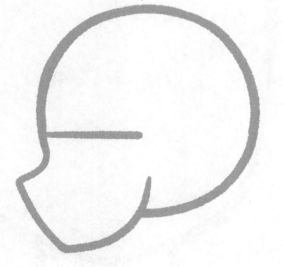

Draw step 3

Trace the outline

1

2

3

4

If you add this eyelash, the eye will be feminine

Draw the eyes above the line

Trace the outline of the eyes

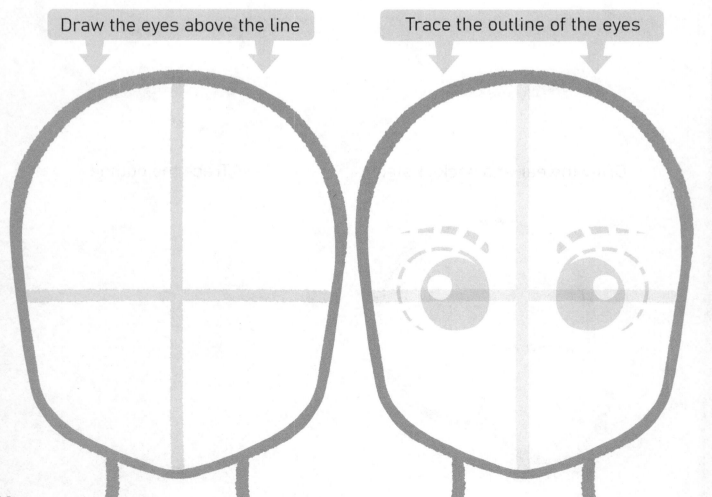

Profile eyes

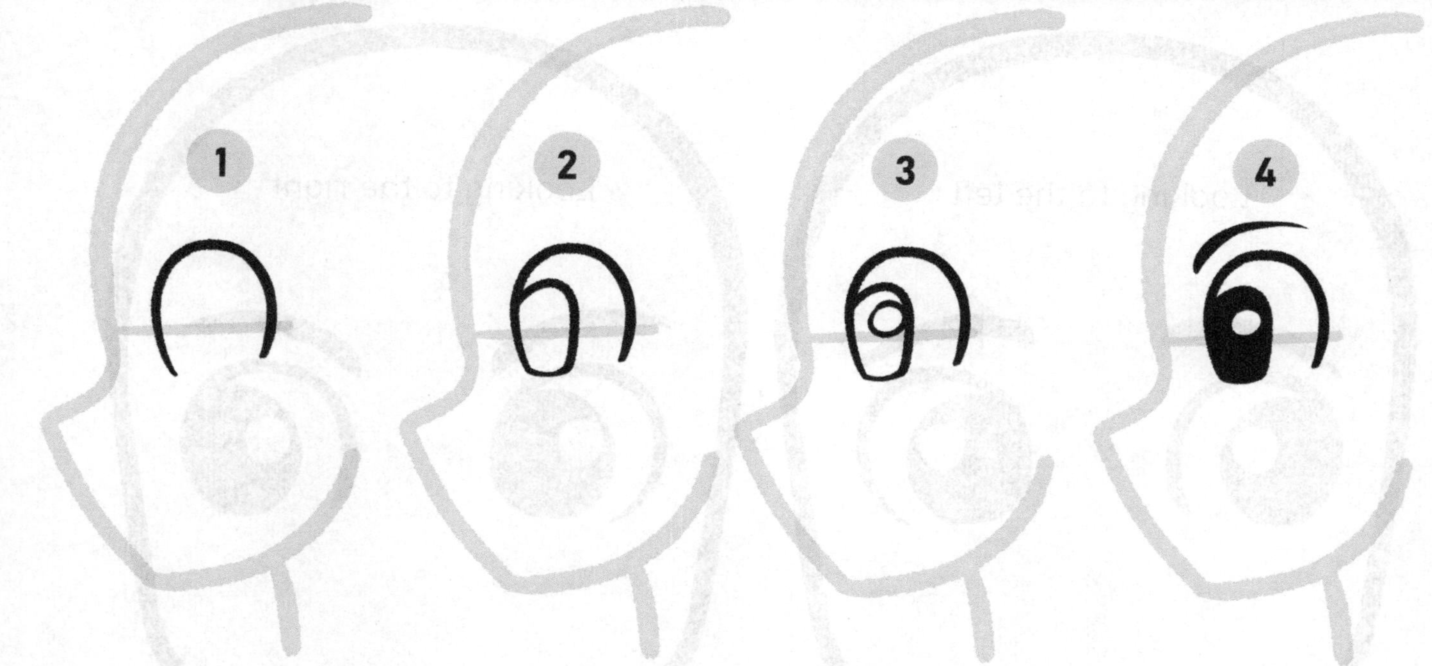
1
2
3
4

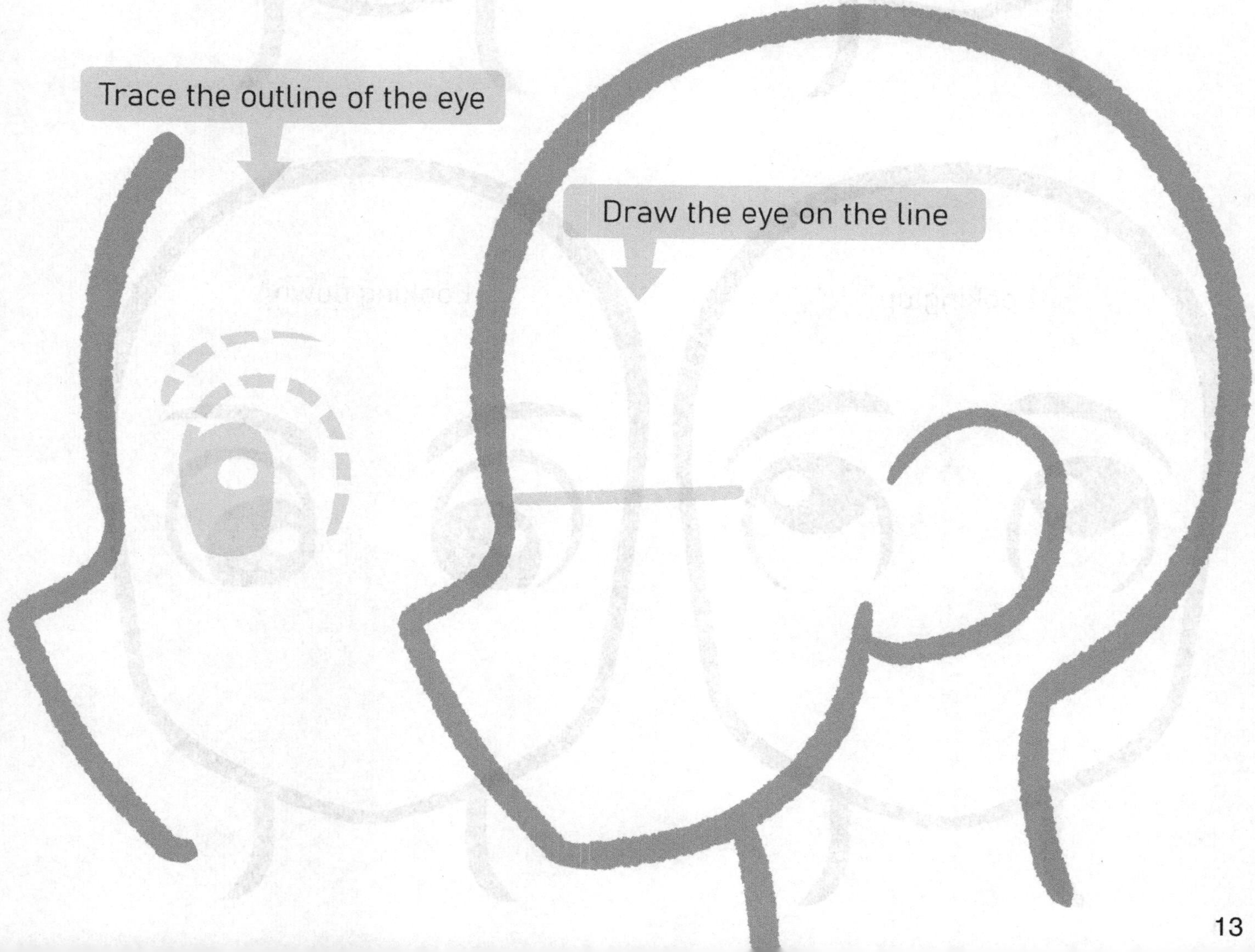
Trace the outline of the eye
Draw the eye on the line

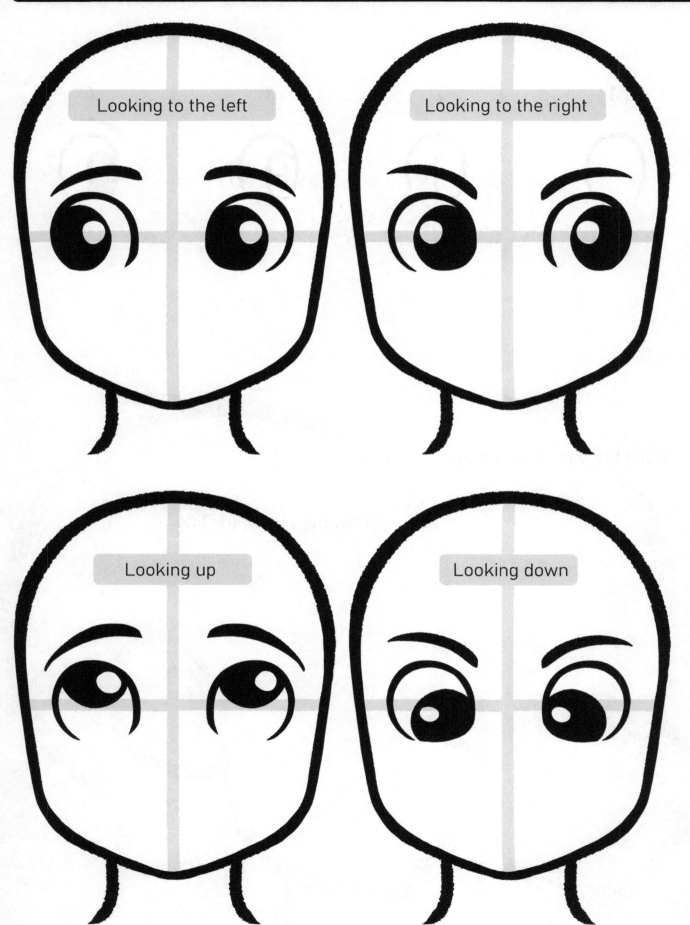

Looking to the left

Looking to the right

Looking up

Looking down

Draw the pupils

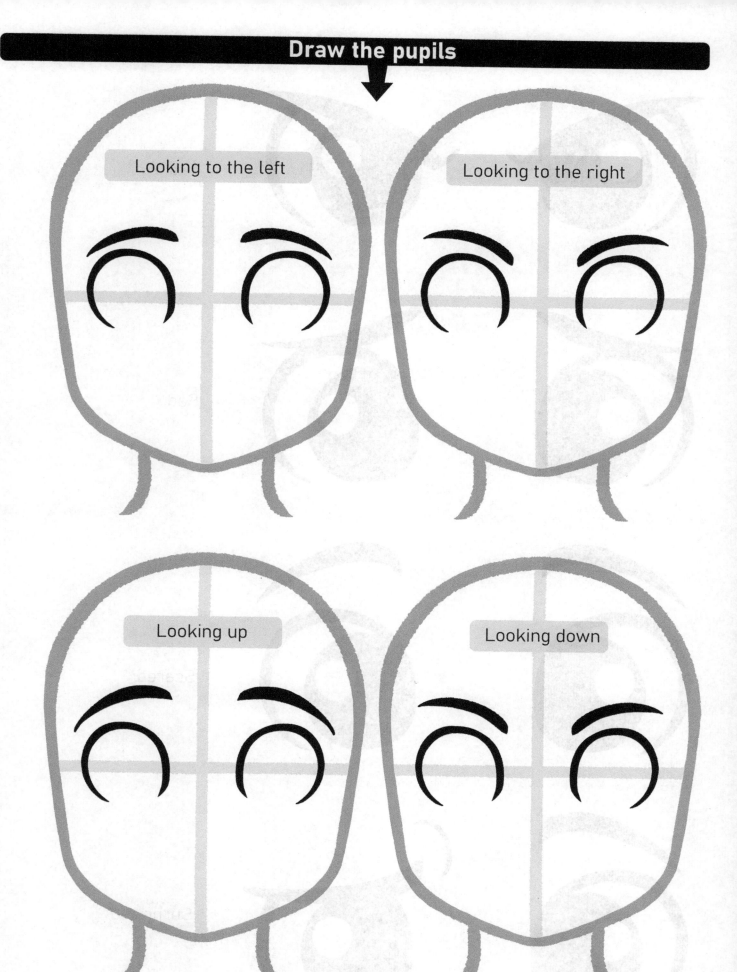

Looking to the left

Looking to the right

Looking up

Looking down

15

Angry

Sad

Scared

Surprised

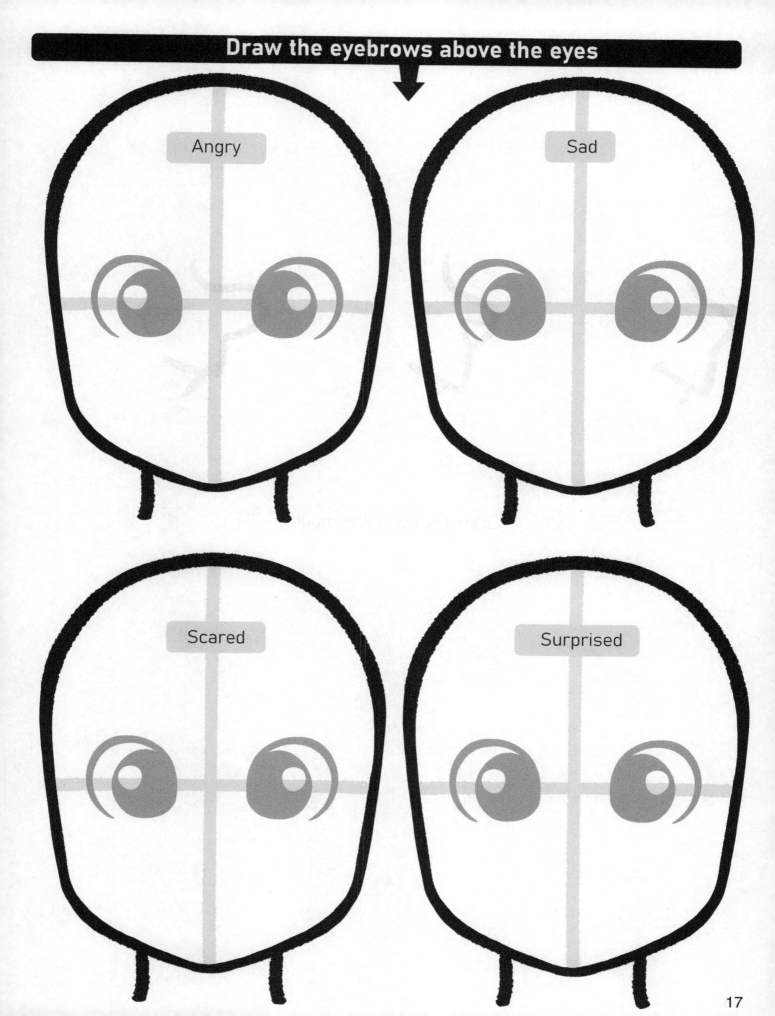

Draw the eyebrows above the eyes

Angry

Sad

Scared

Surprised

Draw the nose and mouth

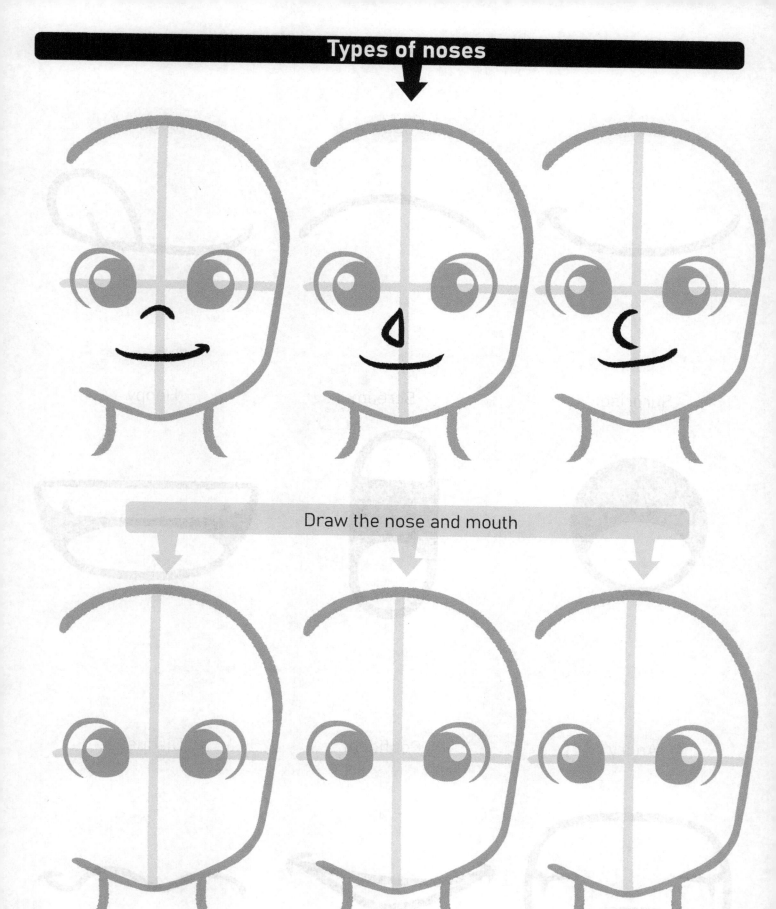

Draw the nose and mouth

Types of mouths

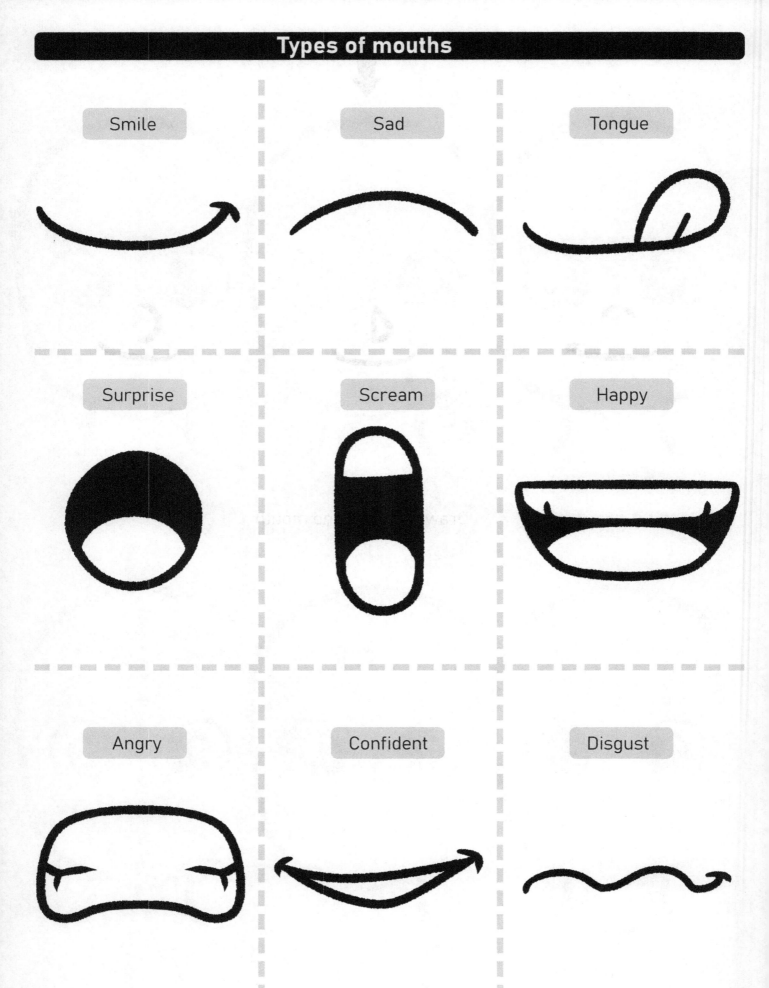

Smile

Sad

Tongue

Surprise

Scream

Happy

Angry

Confident

Disgust

Draw the mouths

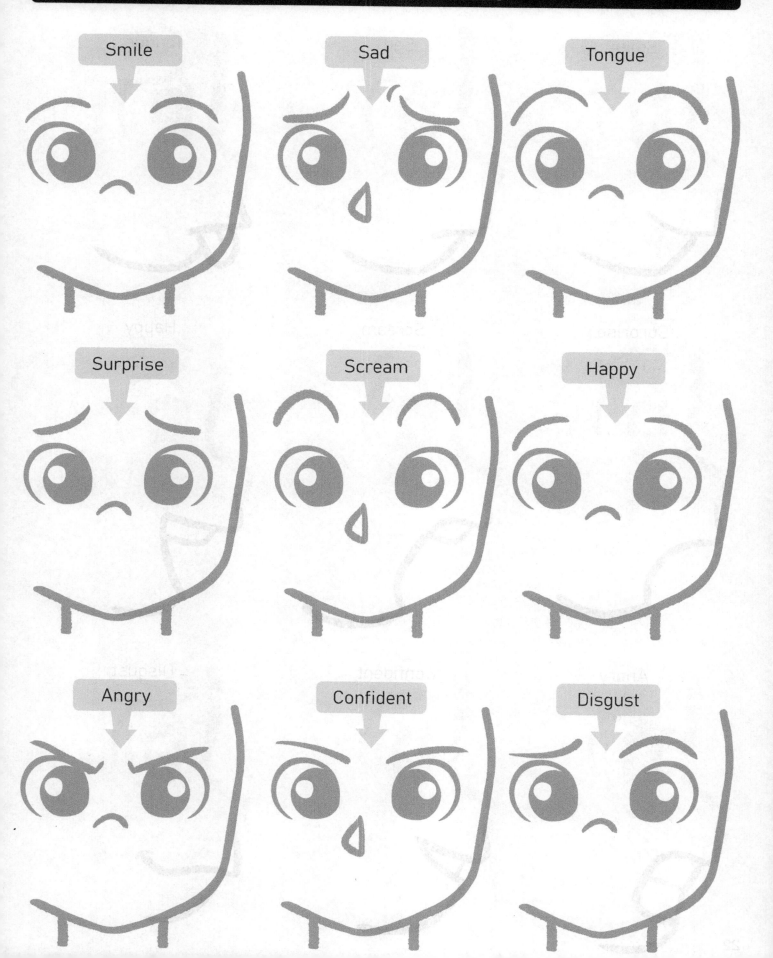

Types of profile mouths

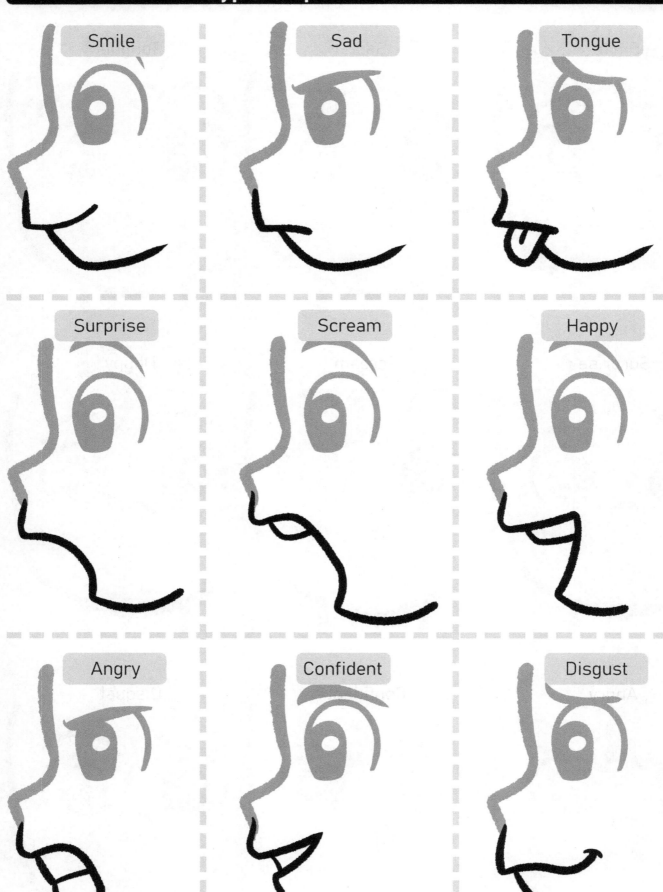

Draw the mouths

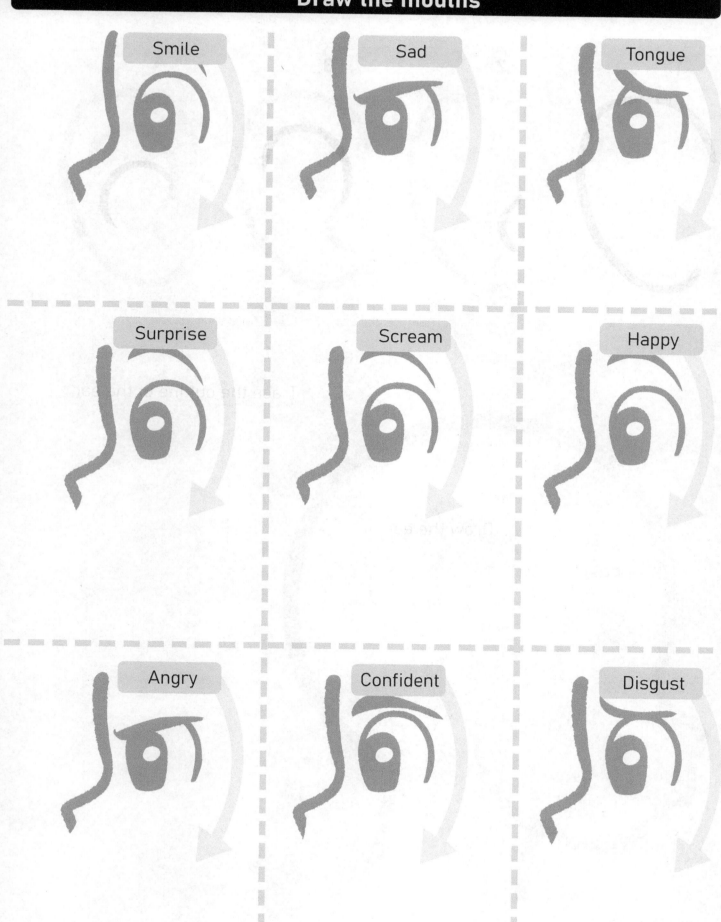

Smile

Sad

Tongue

Surprise

Scream

Happy

Angry

Confident

Disgust

23

Ear (side view of the head)

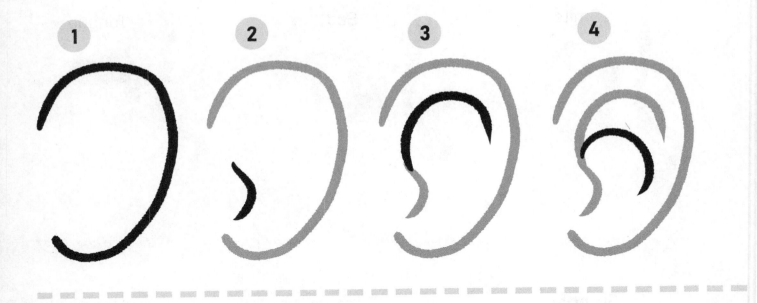

1 2 3 4

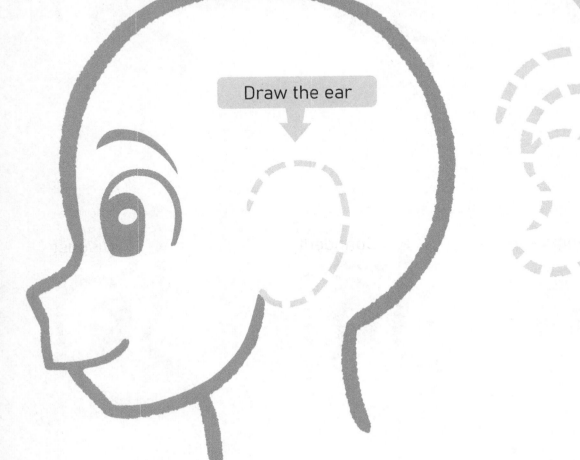

Trace the outline of the ear

Draw the ear

24

Ear (front view of the head)

Draw the ears

Trace the outline of the ear

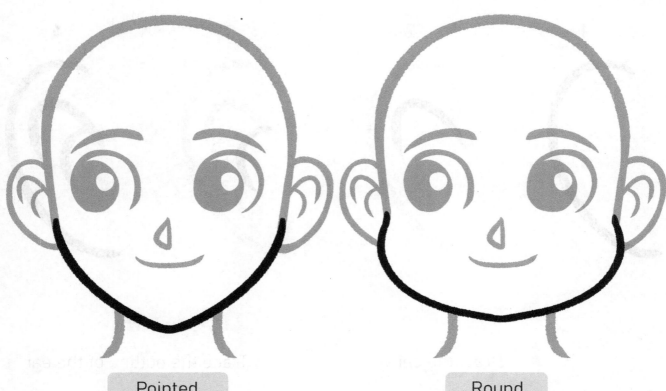

Pointed

Round

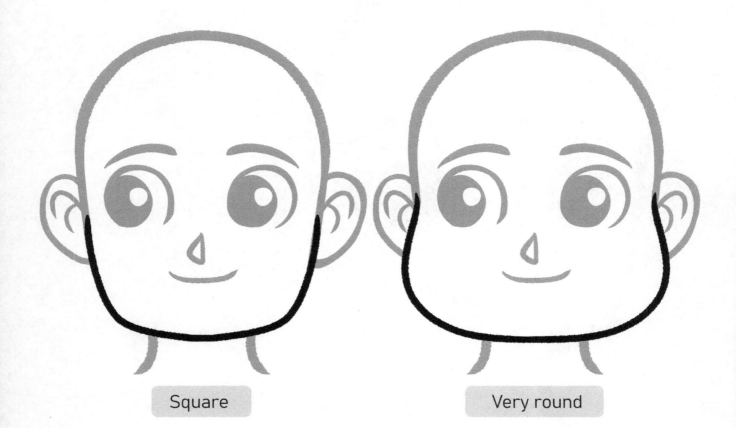

Square

Very round

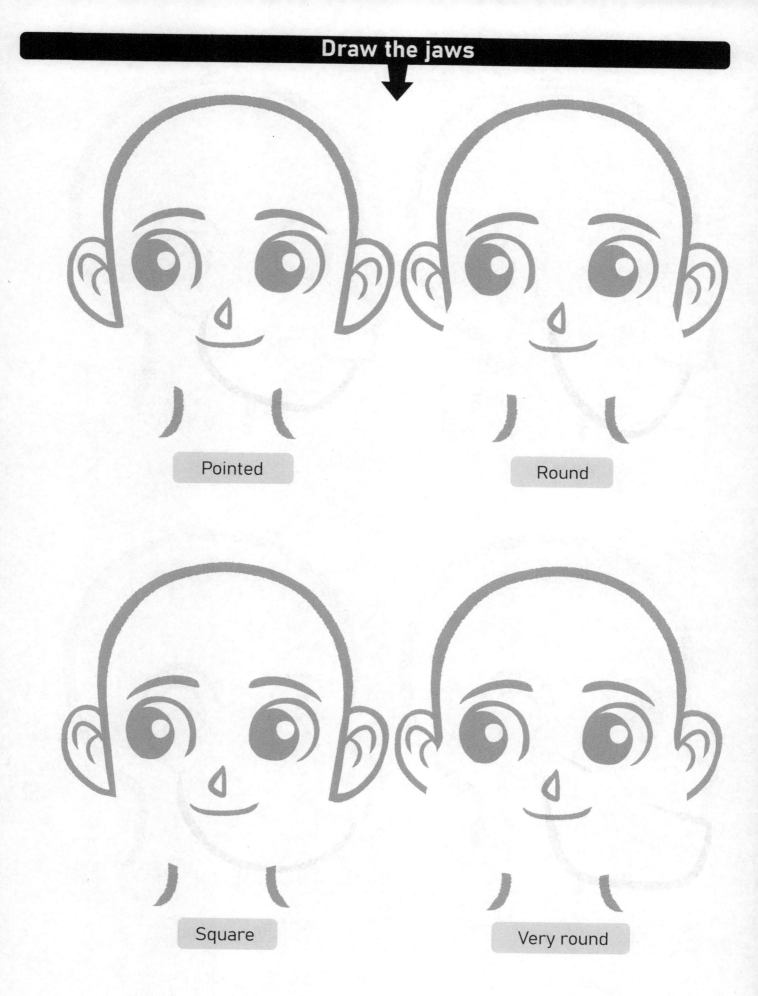

Pointed

Round

Square

Very round

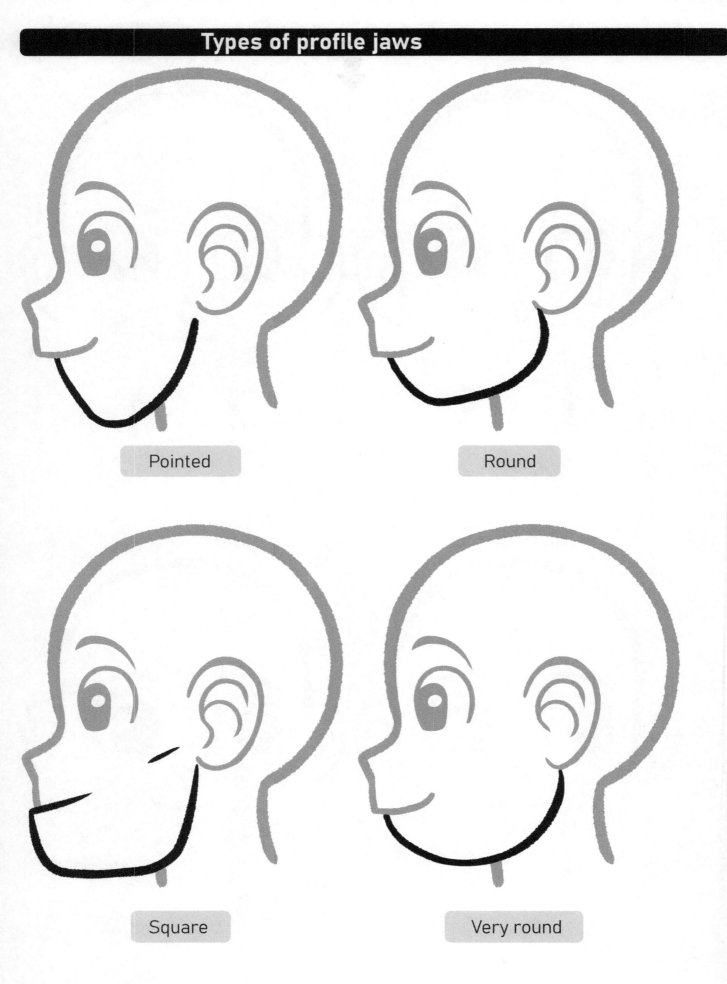

Pointed

Round

Square

Very round

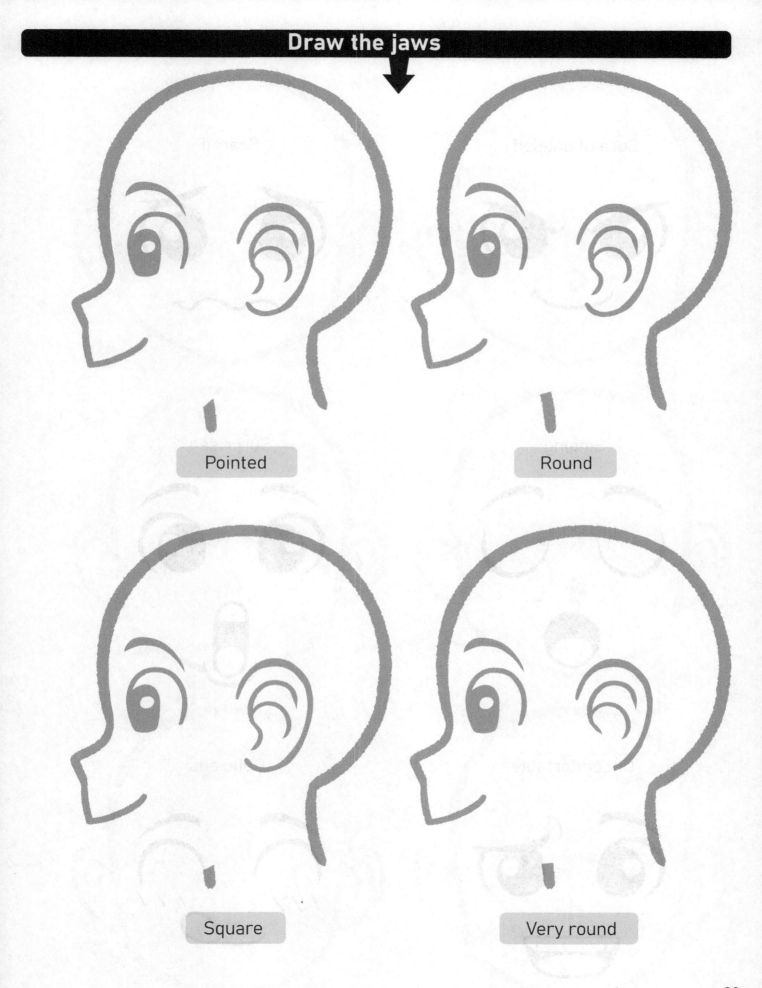

Pointed

Round

Square

Very round

Facial expressions

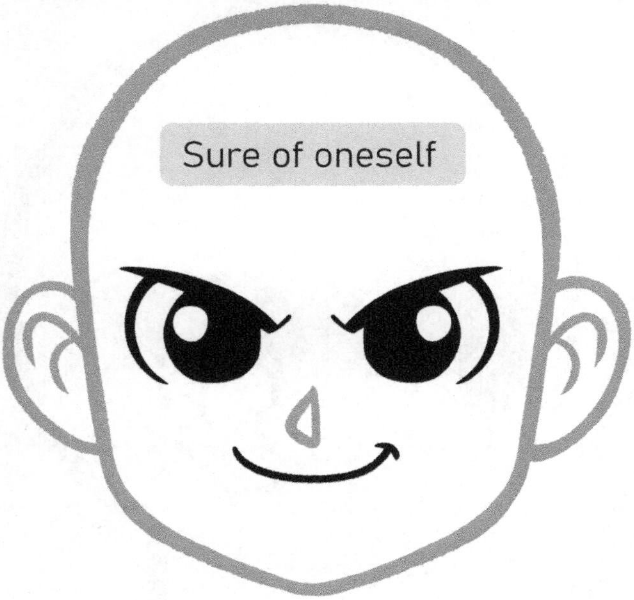
Sure of oneself

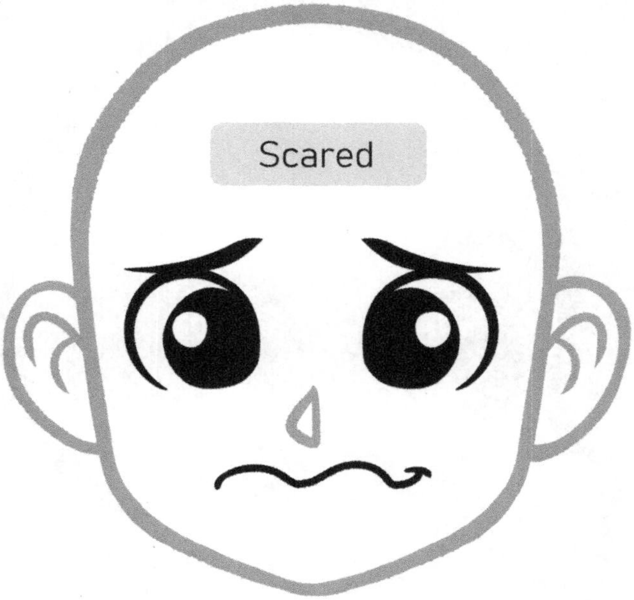
Scared

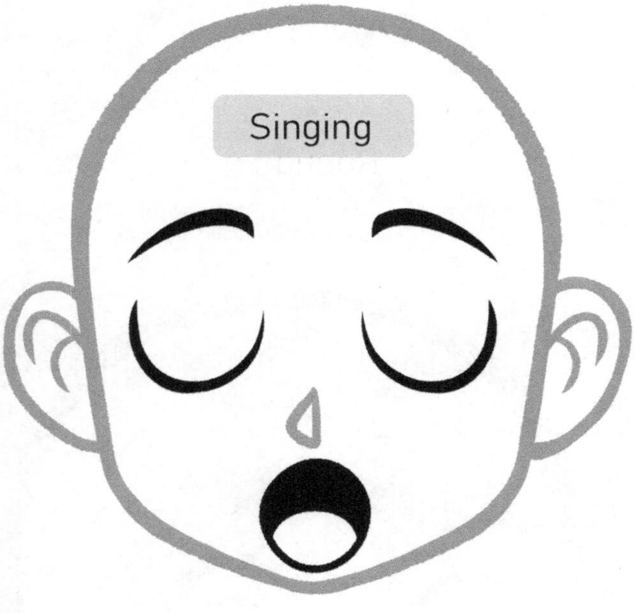
Singing

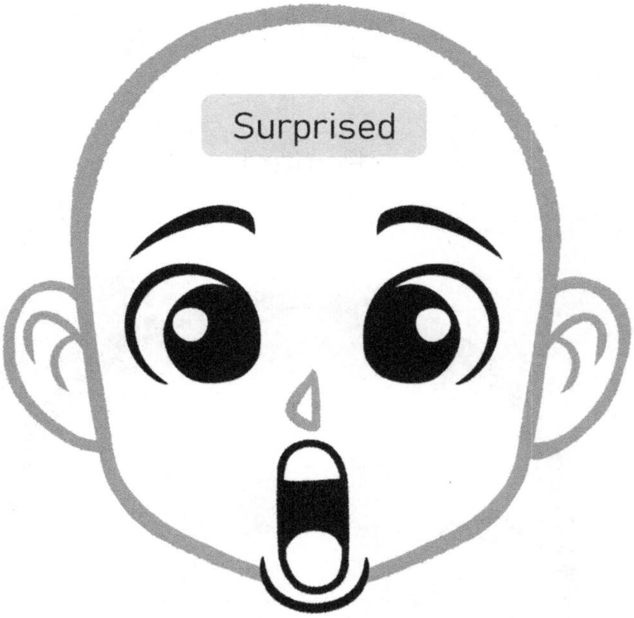
Surprised

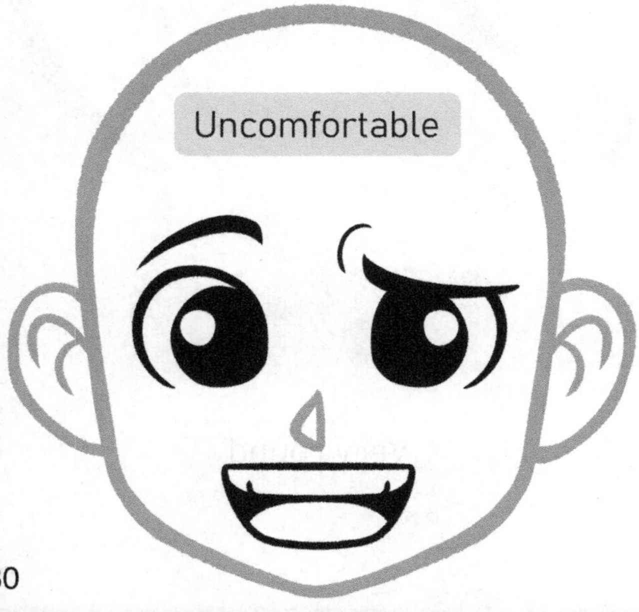
Uncomfortable

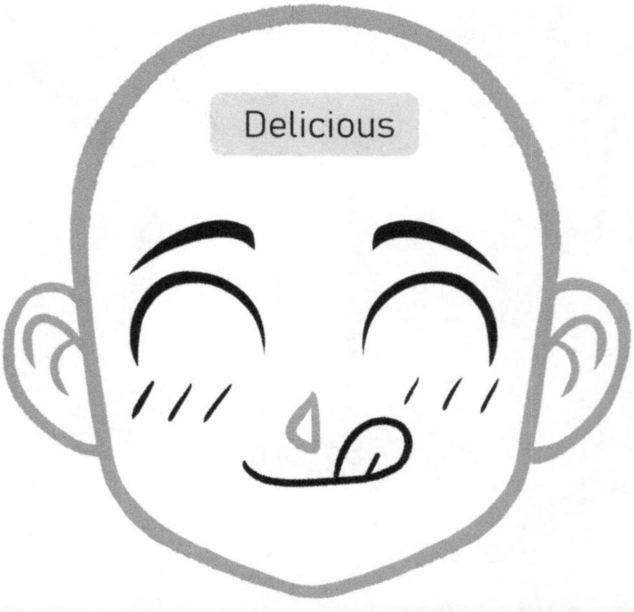
Delicious

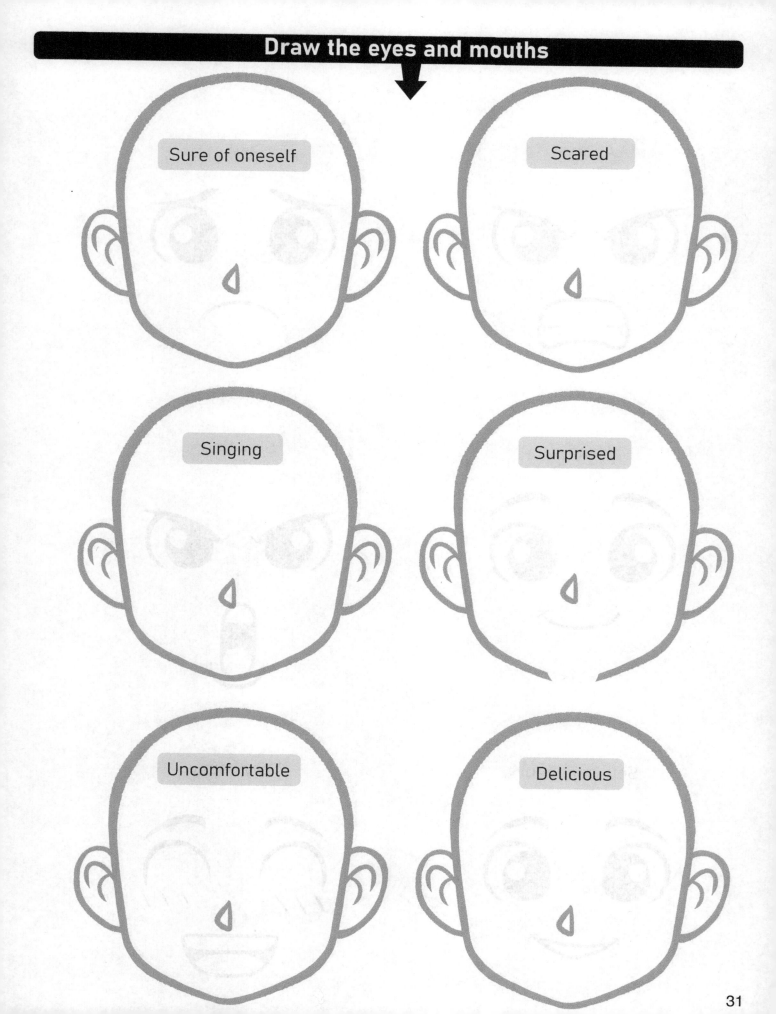

Sure of oneself

Scared

Singing

Surprised

Uncomfortable

Delicious

Facial expressions

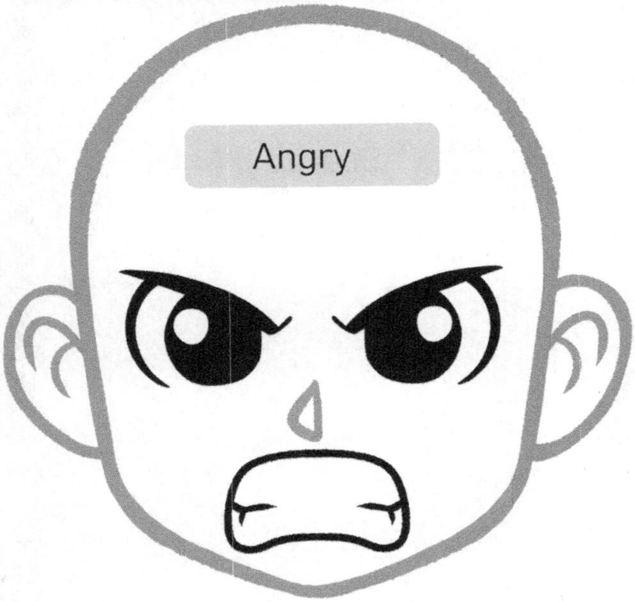
Angry

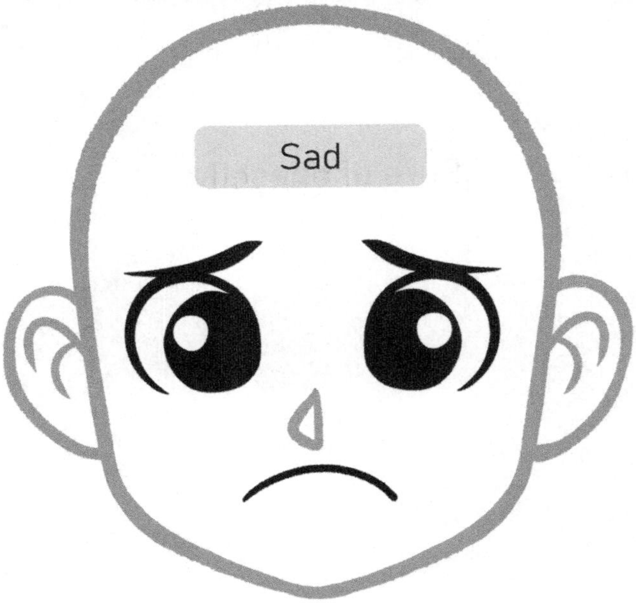
Sad

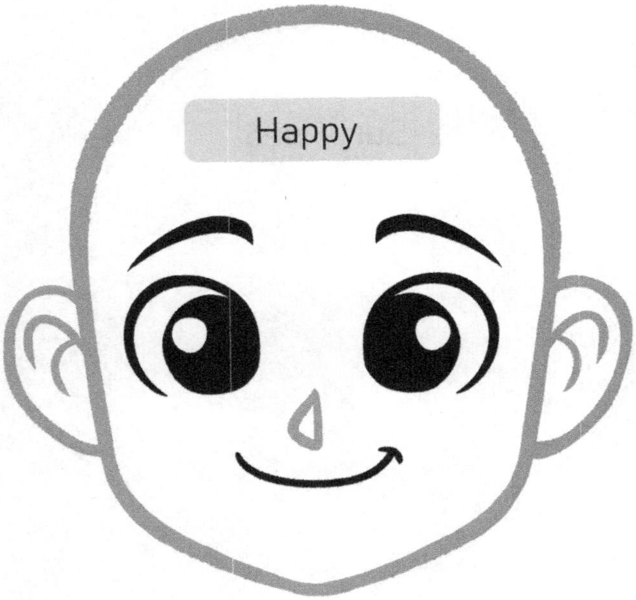
Happy

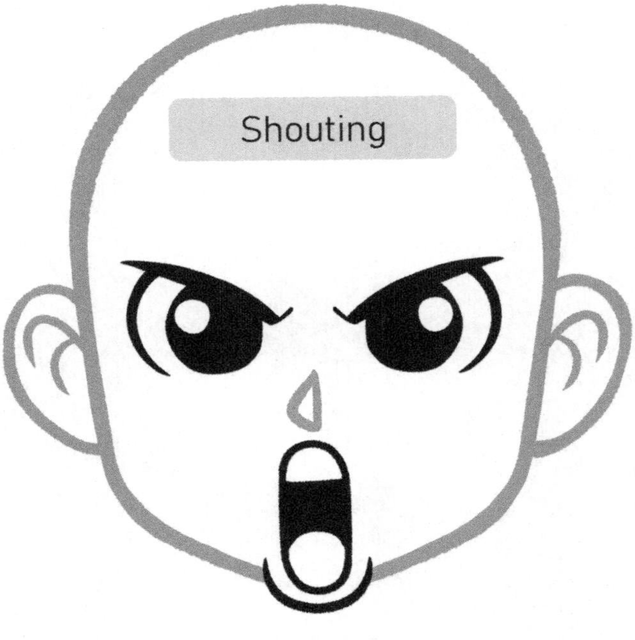
Shouting

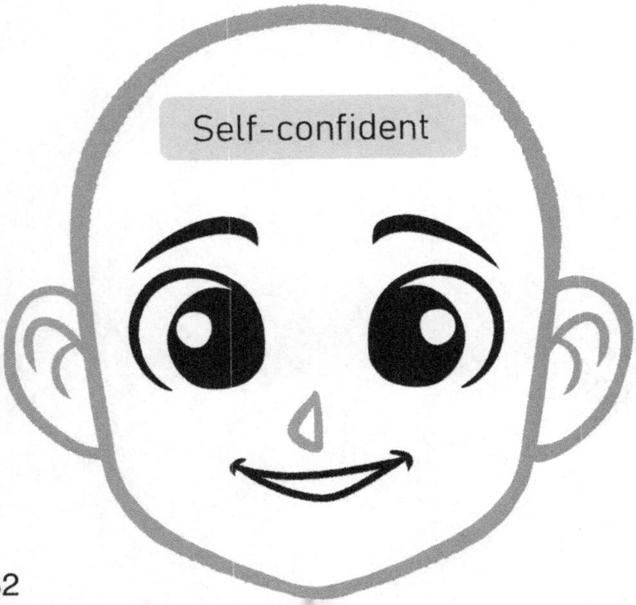
Self-confident

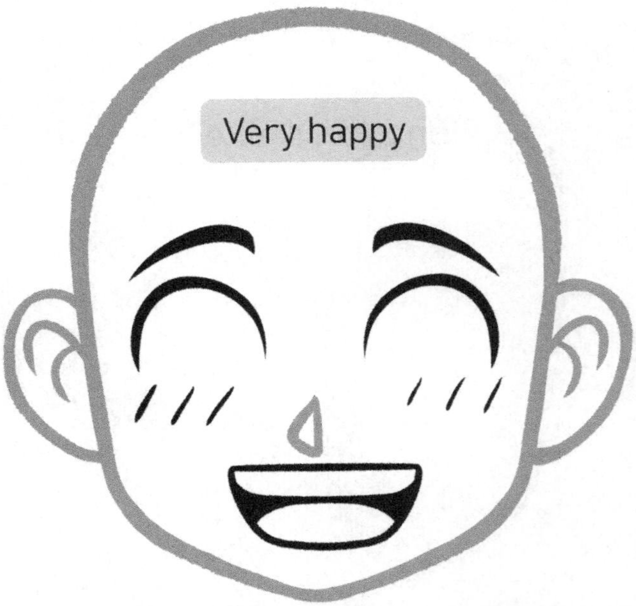
Very happy

Draw the eyes and mouths

Angry

Sad

Happy

Shouting

Self-confident

Very happy

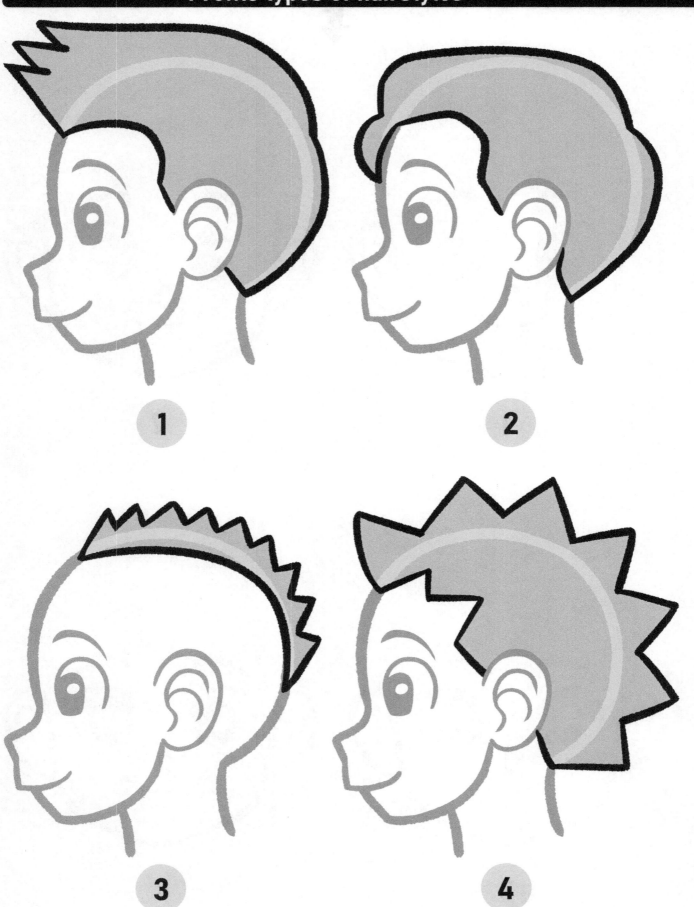

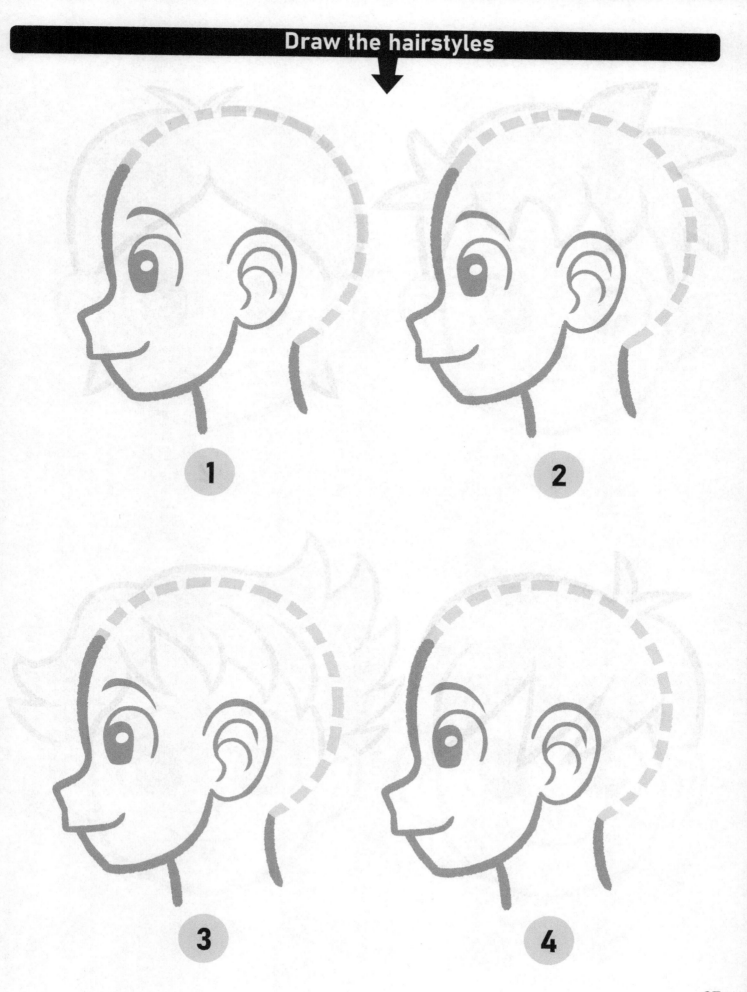

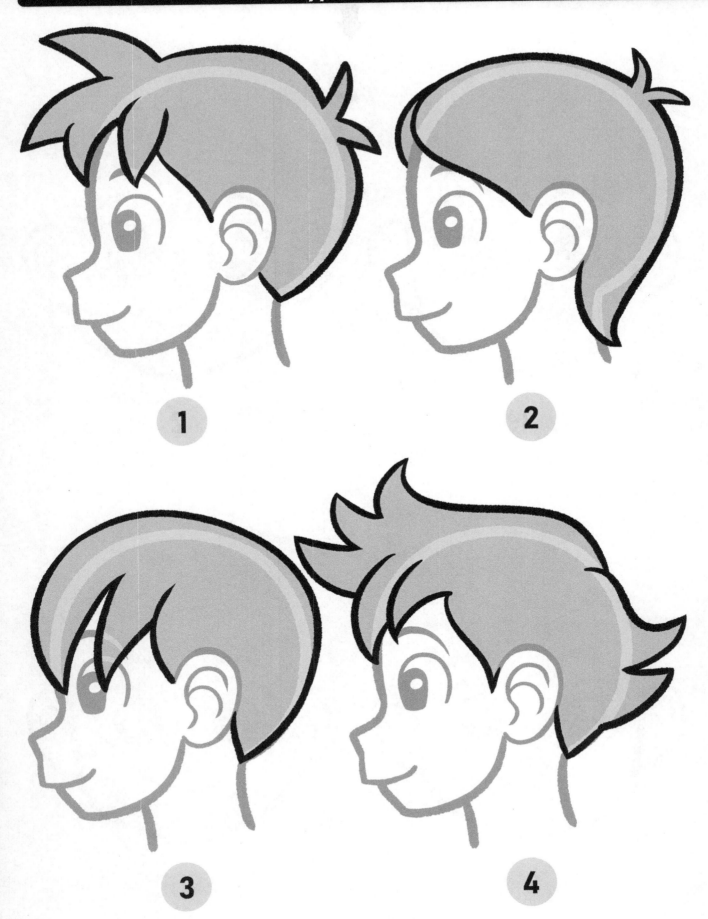

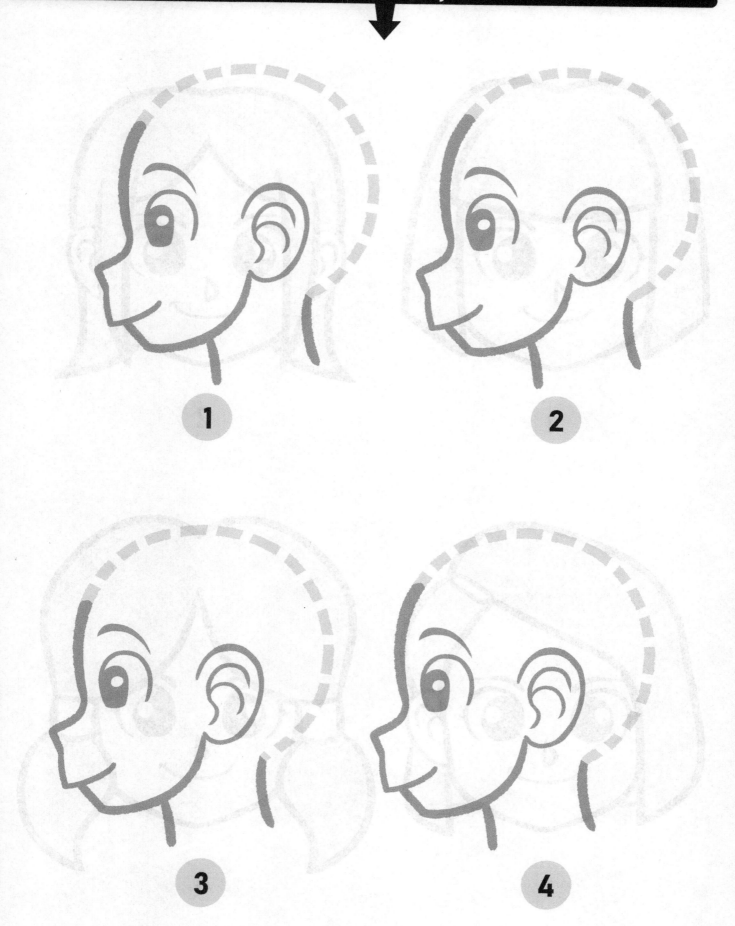

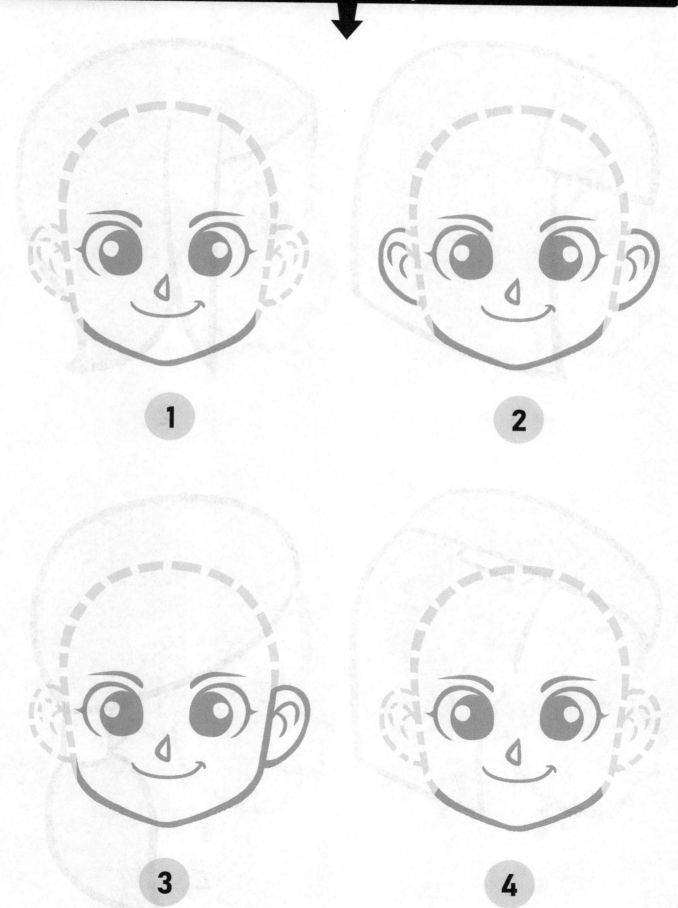

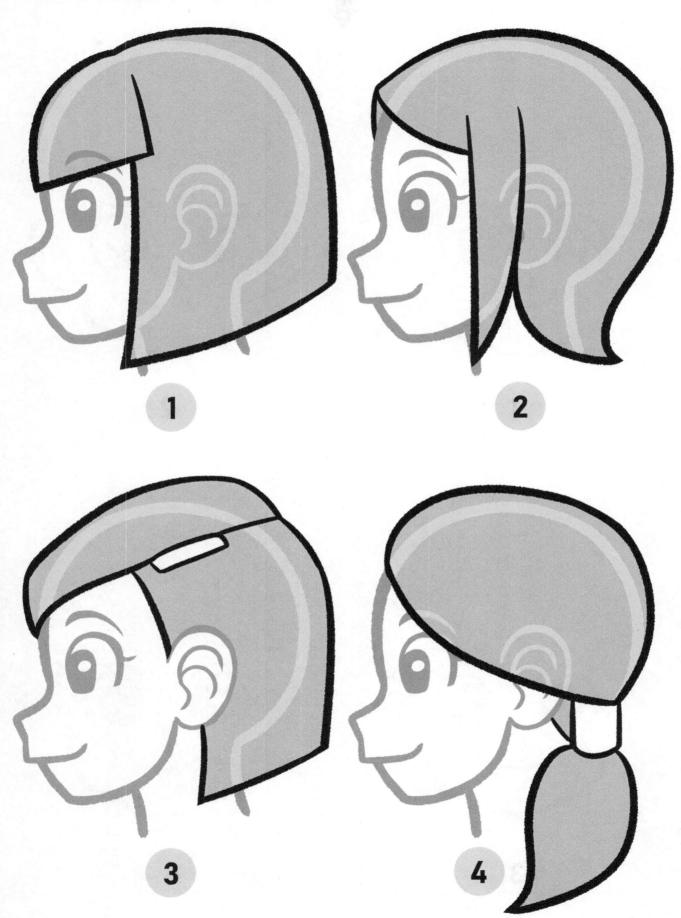

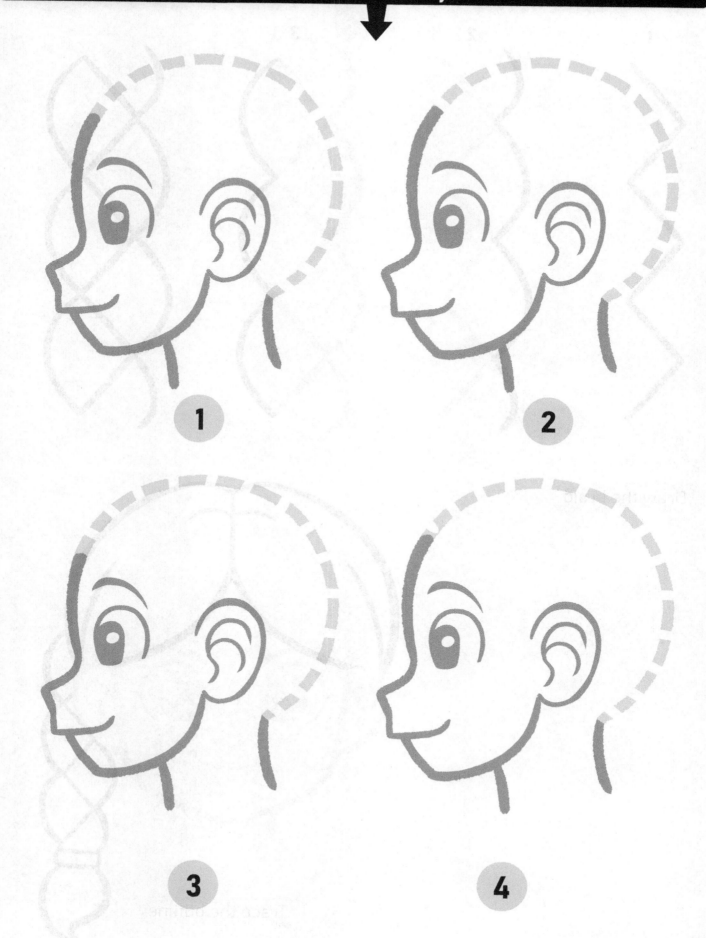

1

2

3

4

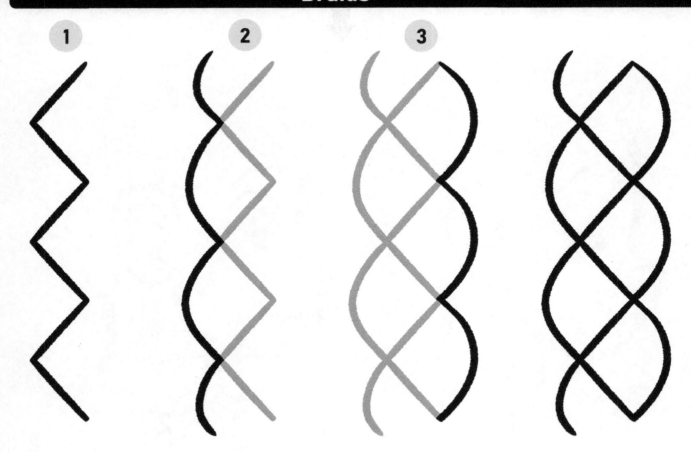

1   **2**   **3**

Draw the braid

Trace the outline

Types of ponytails

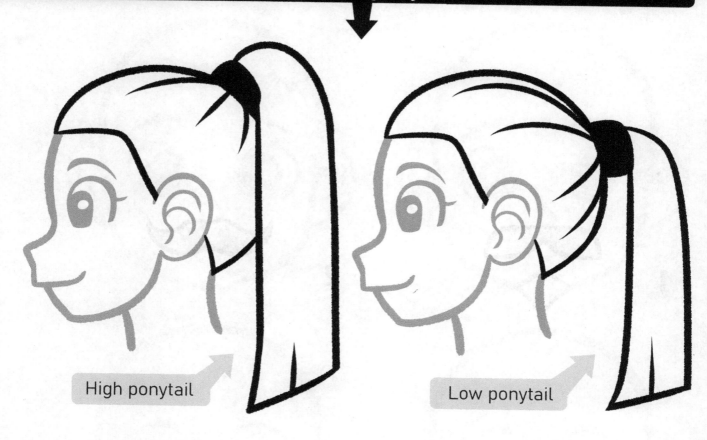

High ponytail

Low ponytail

Draw the ponytails

High ponytail

Low ponytail

47

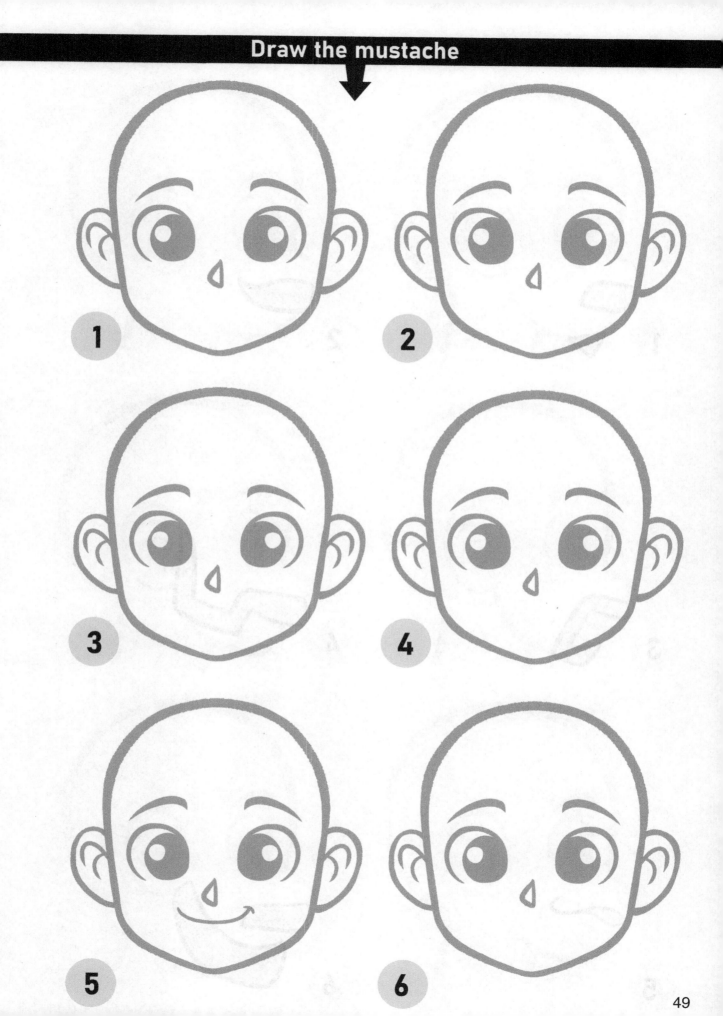

Profile types of mustaches

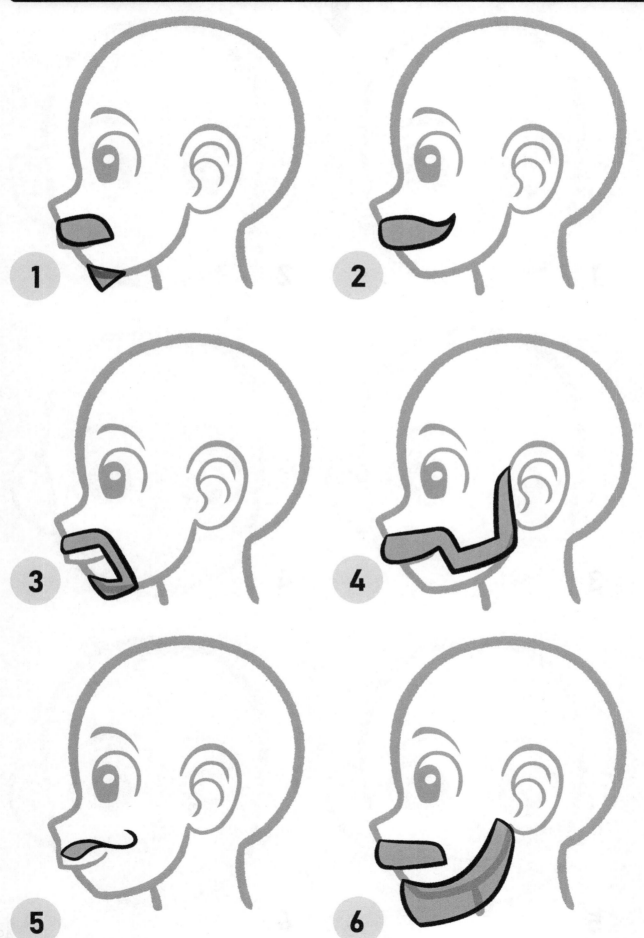

1

2

3

4

5

6

1

2

3

4

5

6

52

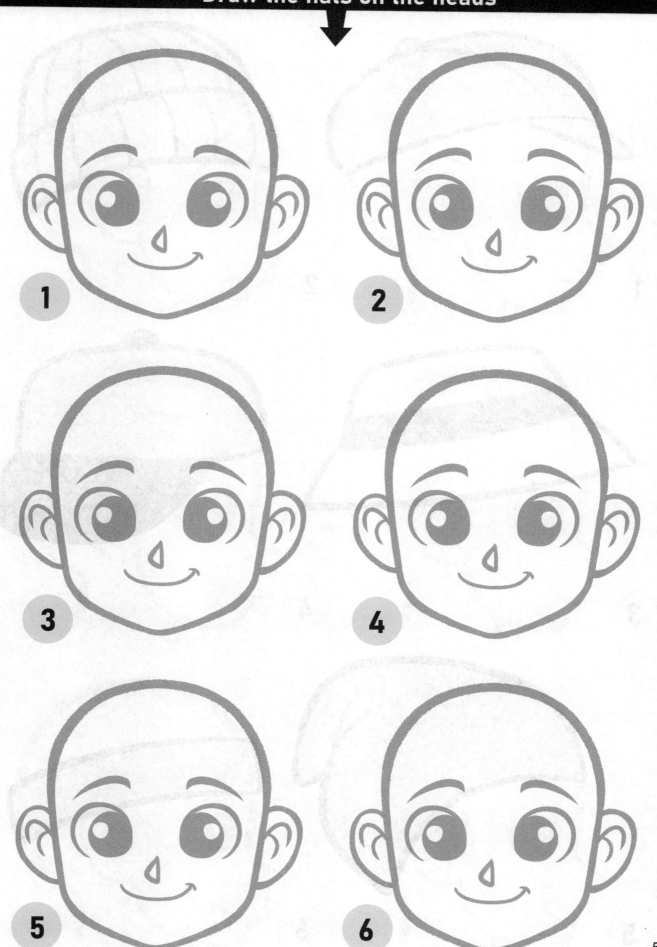

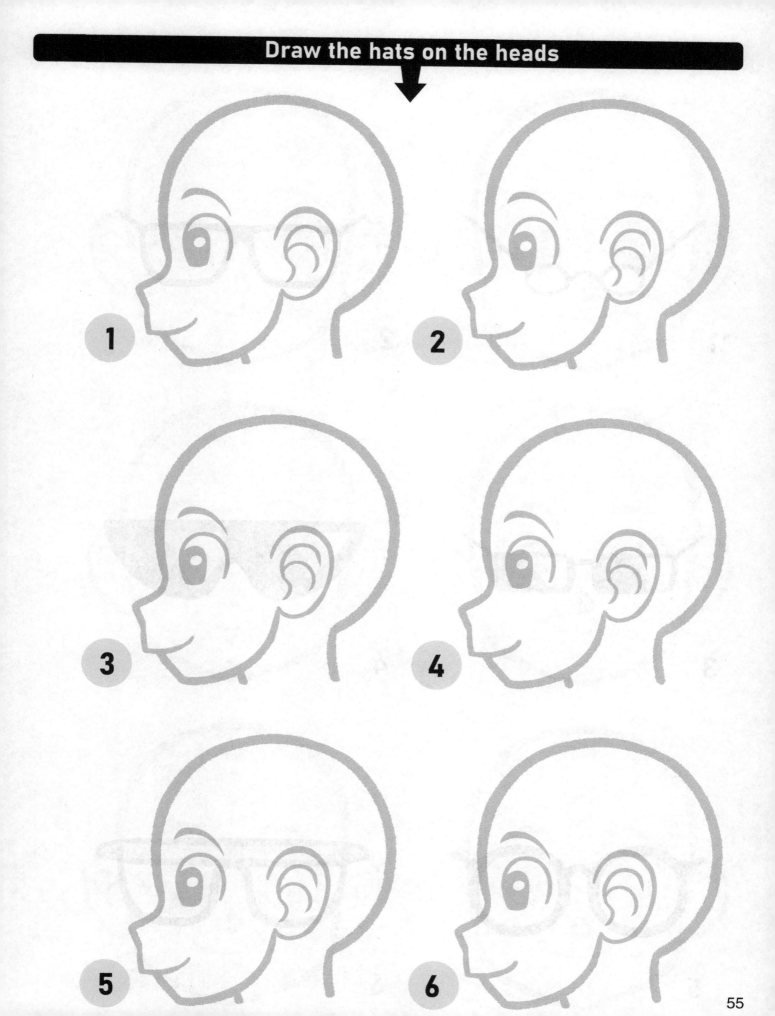

1

2

3

4

5

6

1

2

3

4

5

6

1

2

3

4

5

6

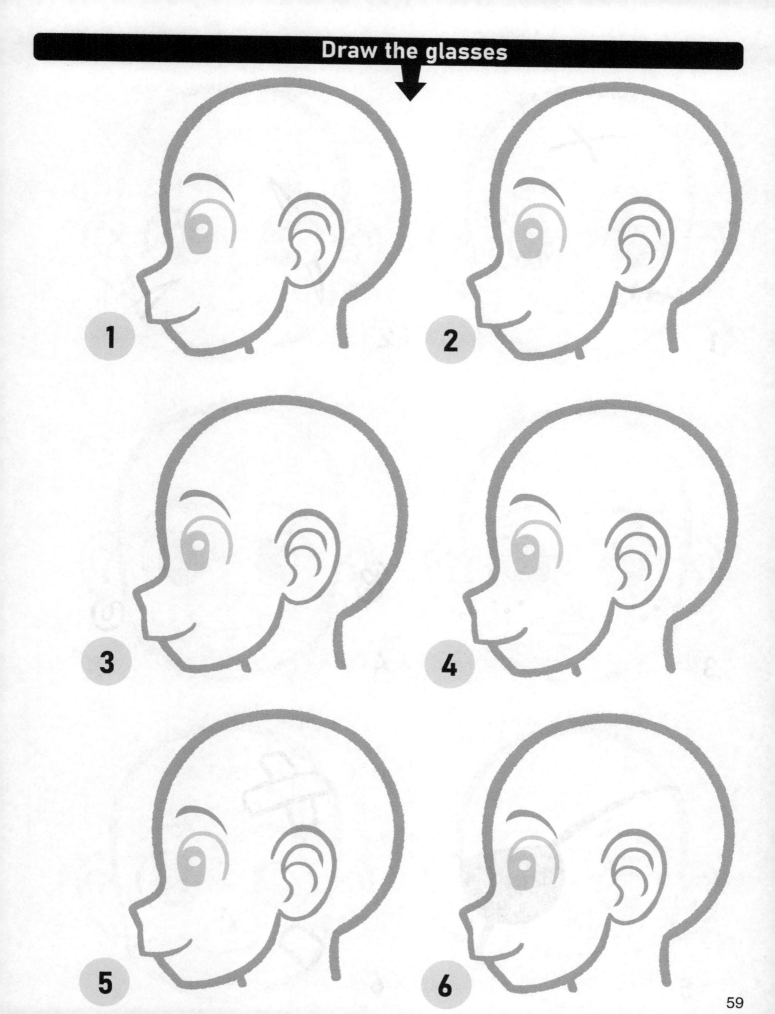

Draw the glasses

59

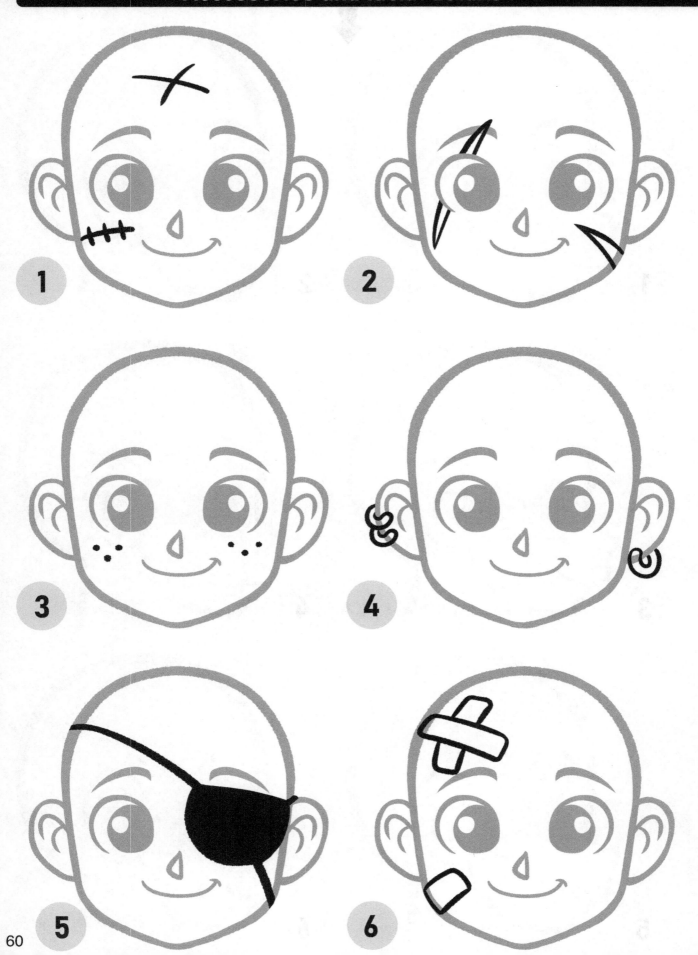

1

2

3

4

5

6

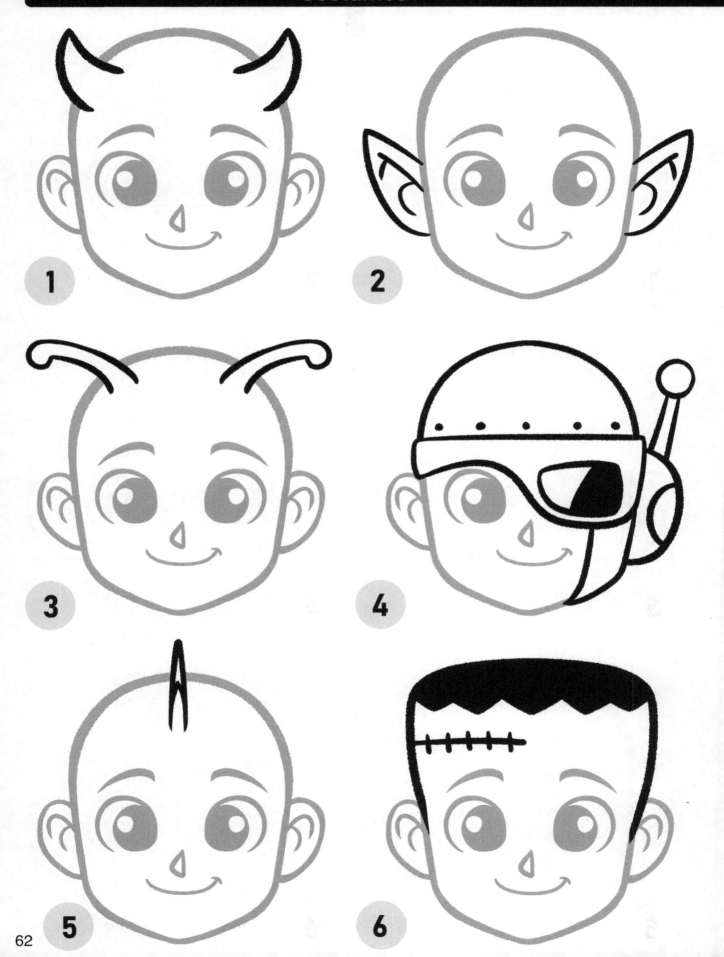

1

2

3

4

5

6

1

2

3

4

5

6

1

2

3

4

5

6

1

2

3

4

5

6

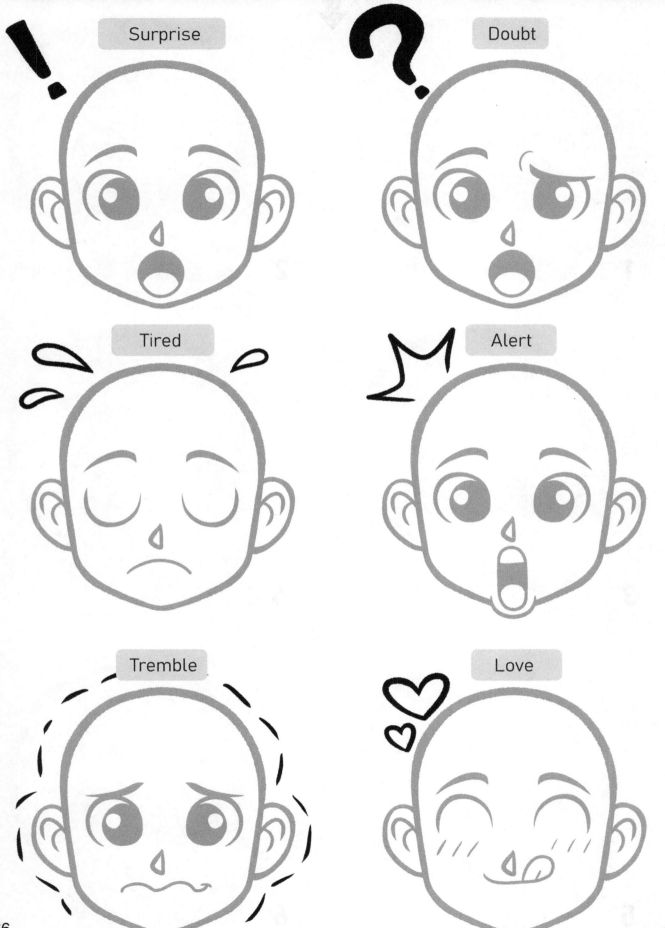

Dizziness

Tension

Joy

Music

Anger

Stress

Body

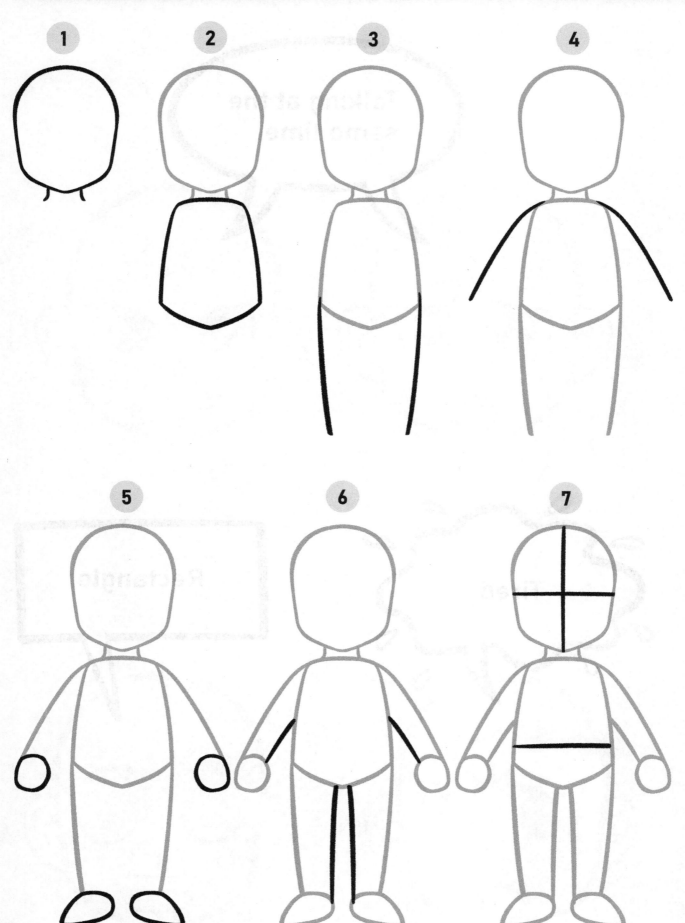

Finish drawing the legs and arms

Draw the arms and legs

Draw the body

Trace the outline of the body

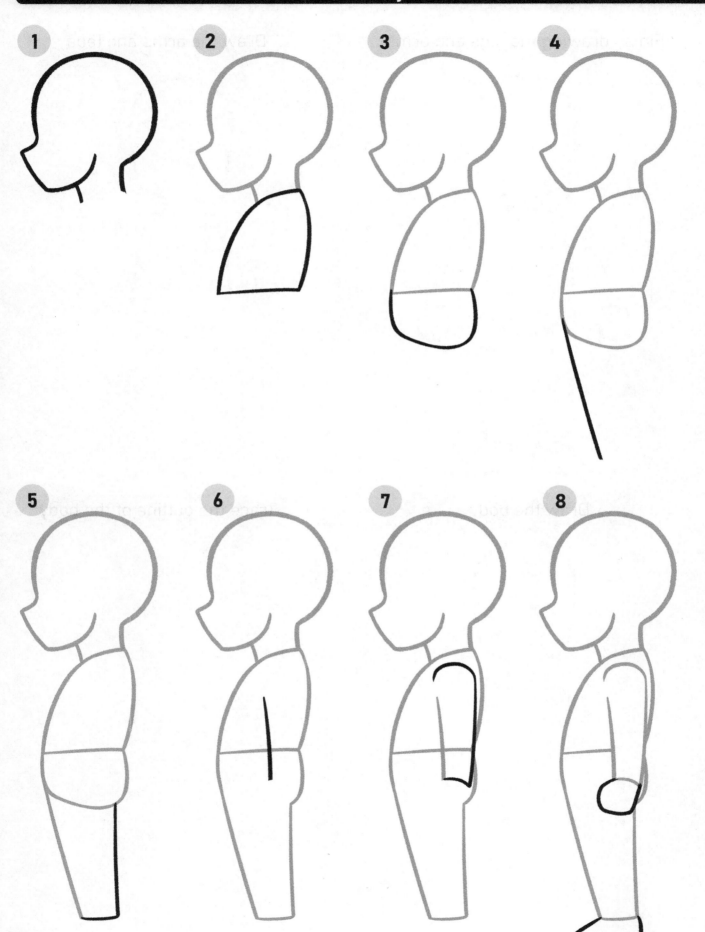

Draw the body in profile

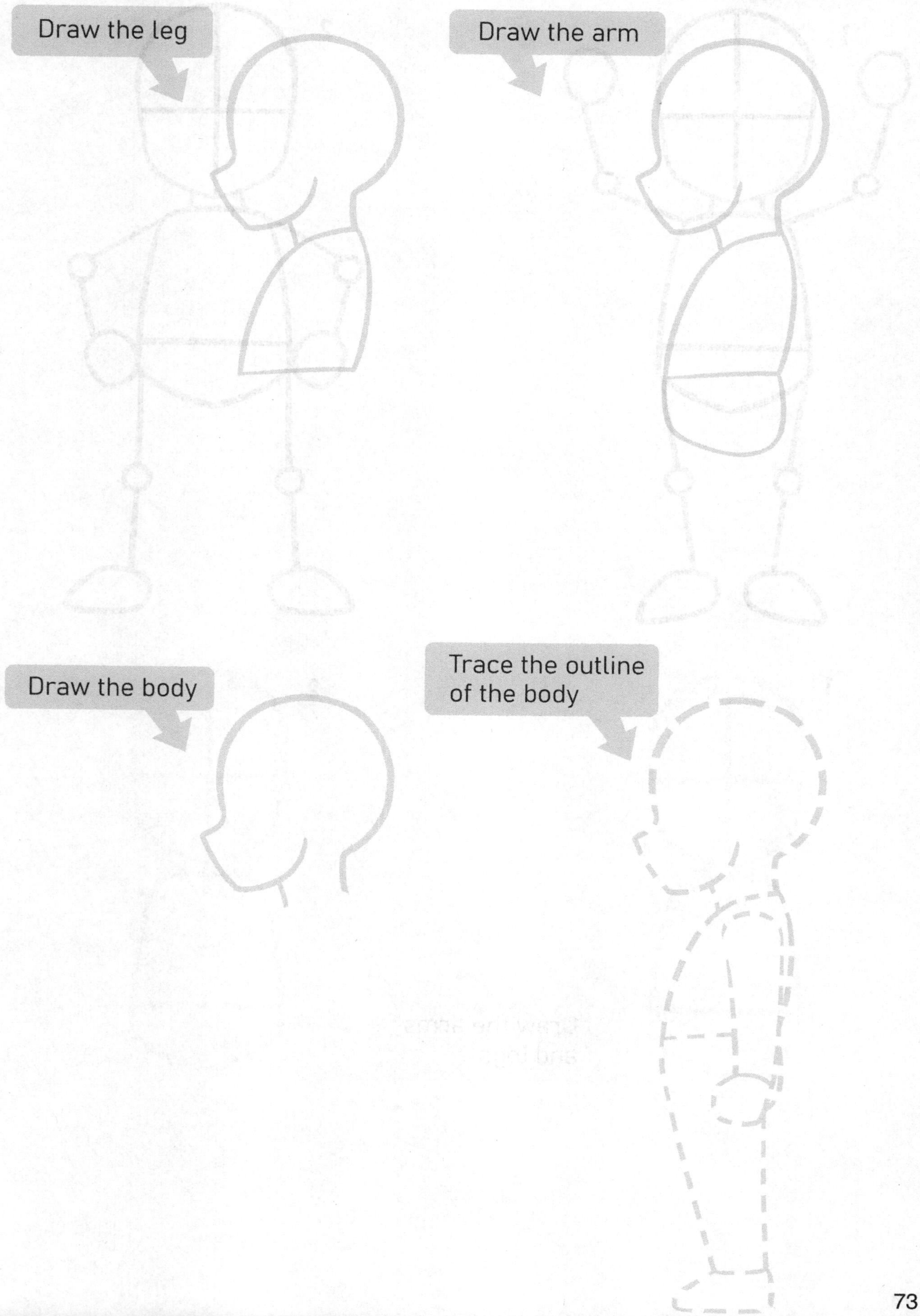
Draw the leg
Draw the arm
Draw the body
Trace the outline of the body

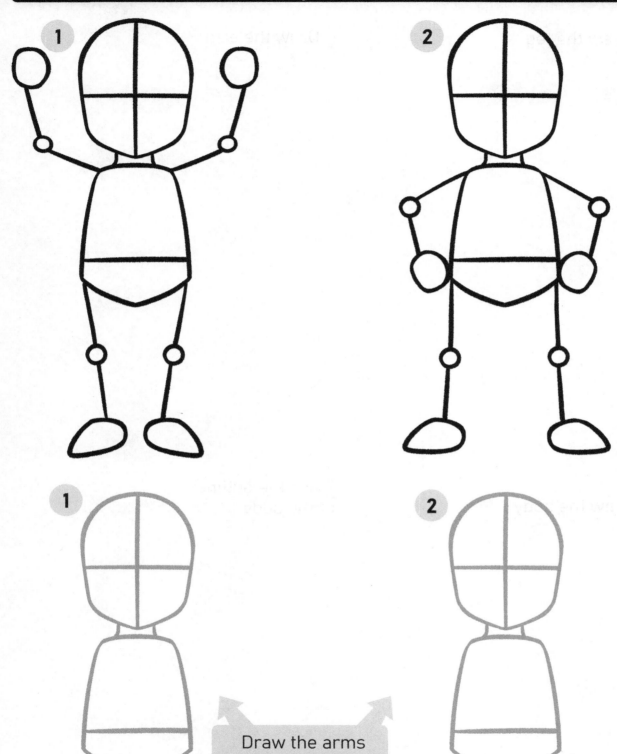

Draw the arms and legs

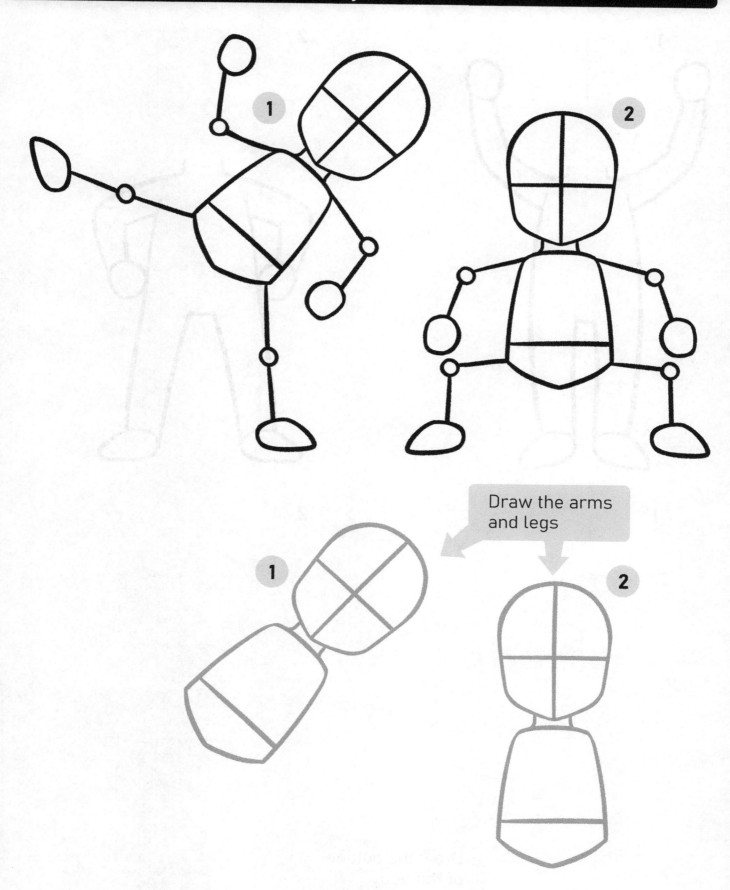

Draw the arms and legs

Draw the outline
of the body

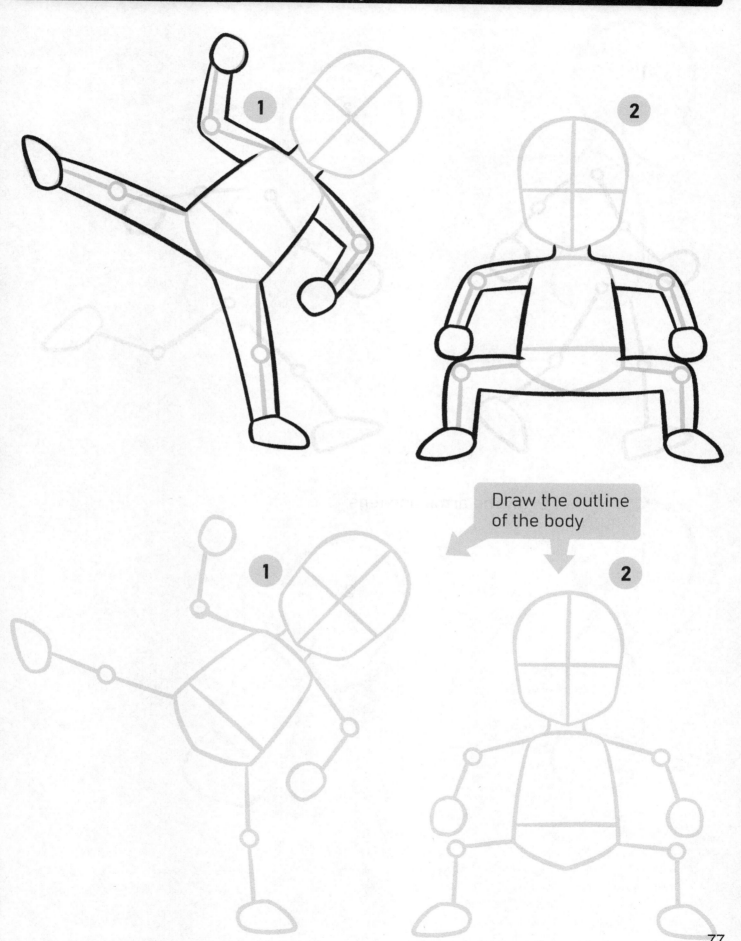

Draw the outline of the body

Draw the arms and legs

Draw the outline of the body

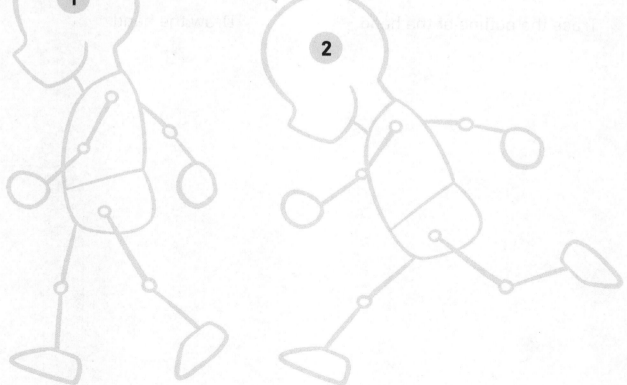

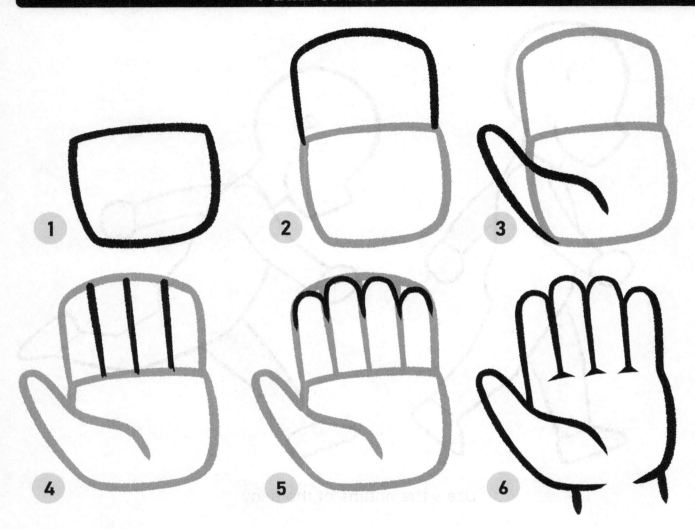

Trace the outline of the hand

Draw the hand

Open palm of hand

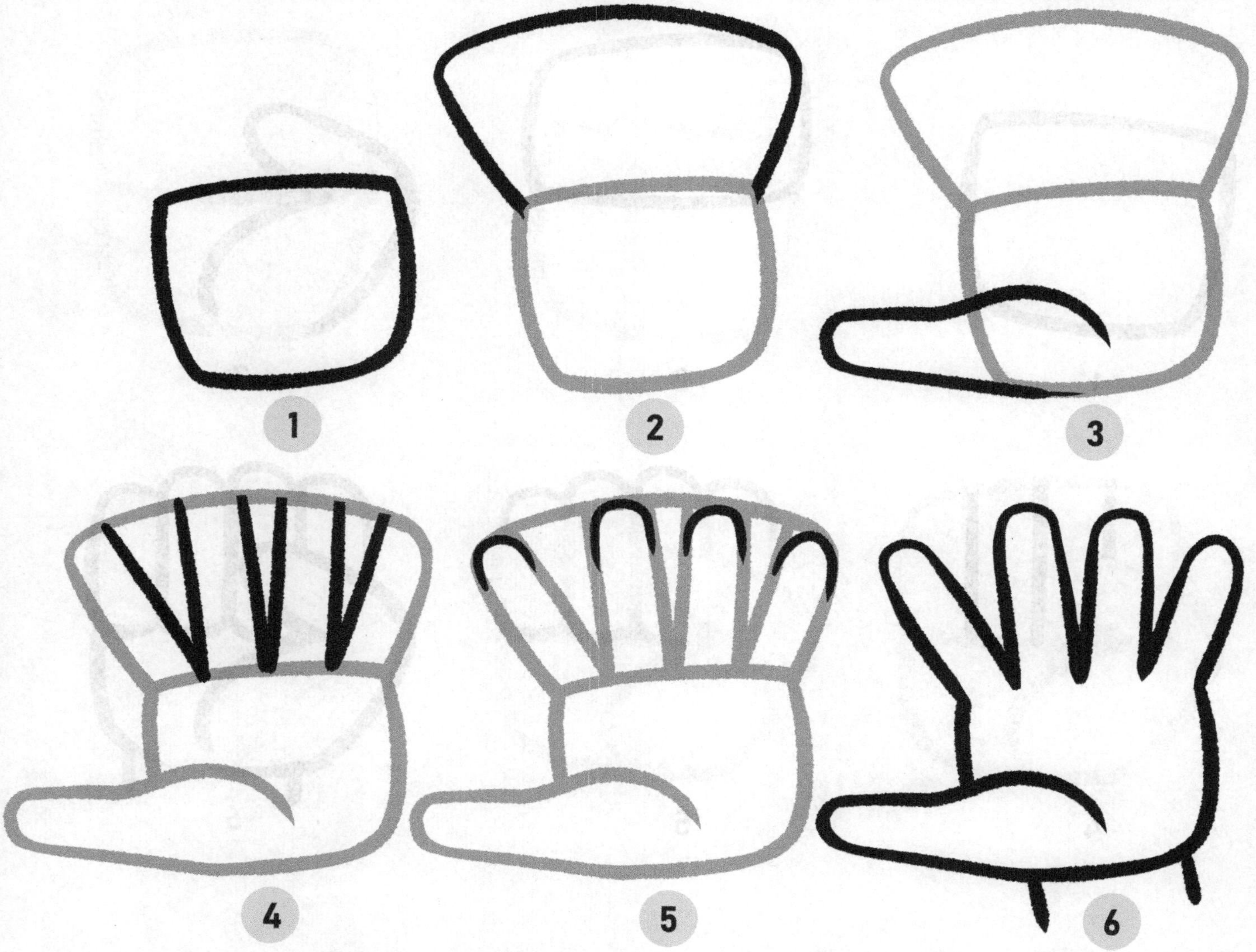

1

2

3

4

5

6

Trace the outline of the hand

Draw the hand

Fist

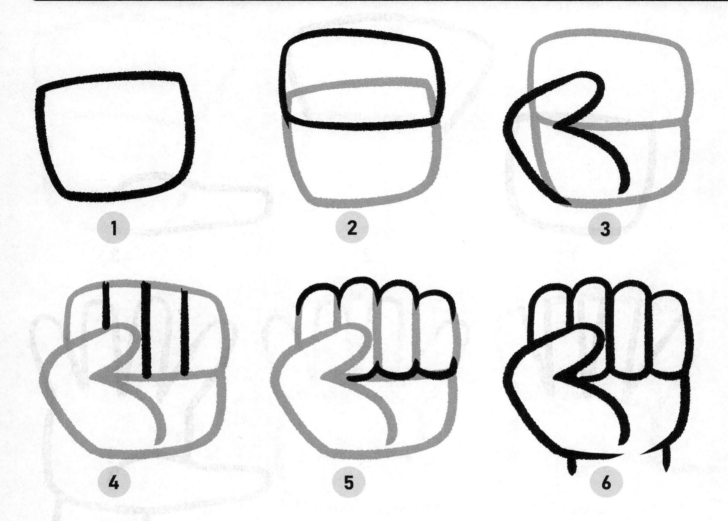

1
2
3
4
5
6

Trace the outline of the fist

Draw the fist

82

Fist

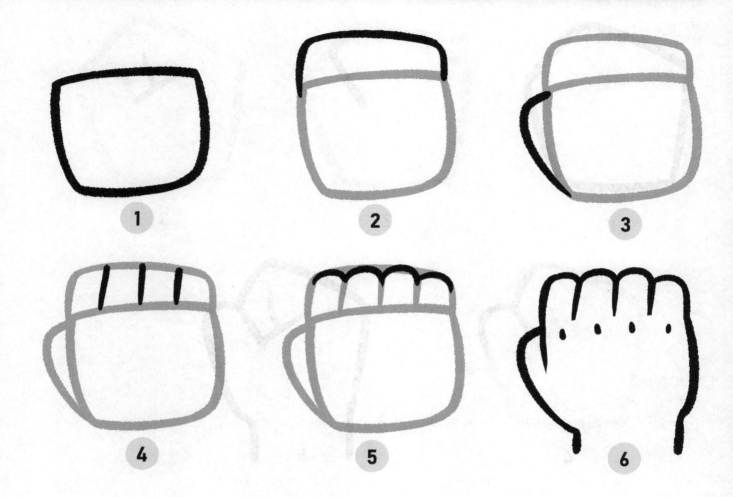

Trace the outline of the fist

Draw the fist

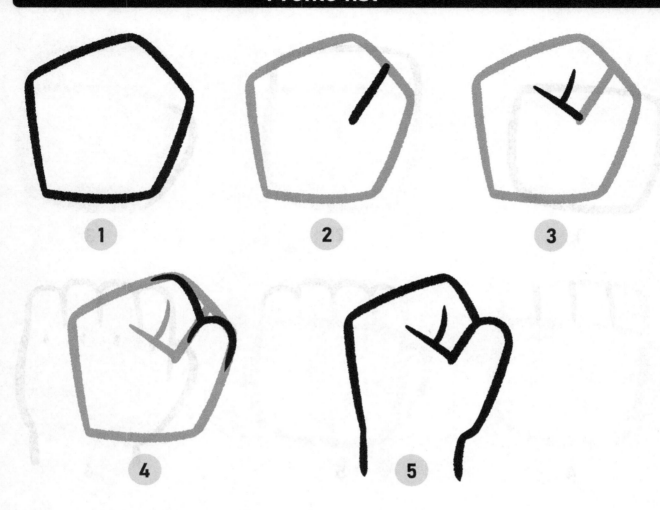

Trace the outline of the fist

Draw the fist

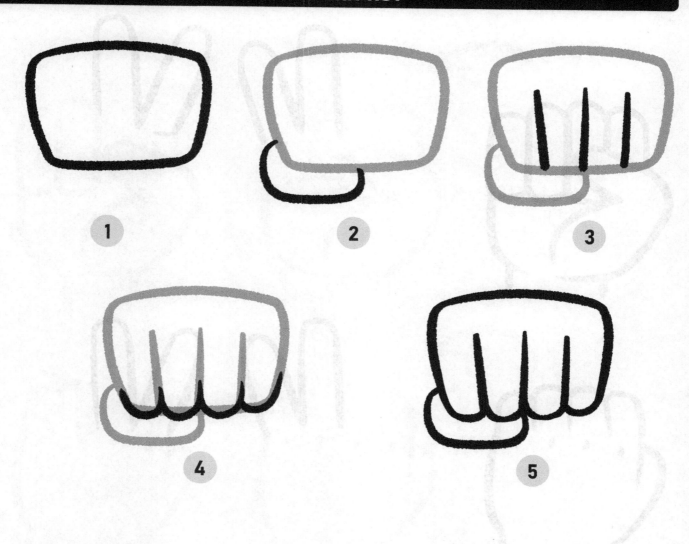

1

2

3

4

5

Trace the outline of the fist

Draw the fist

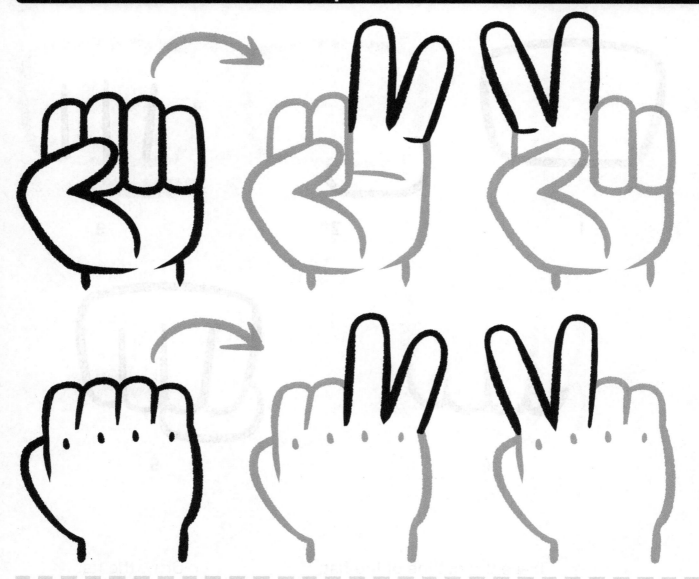

Draw the 2 missing fingers on these hands

Draw the missing fingers on these hands

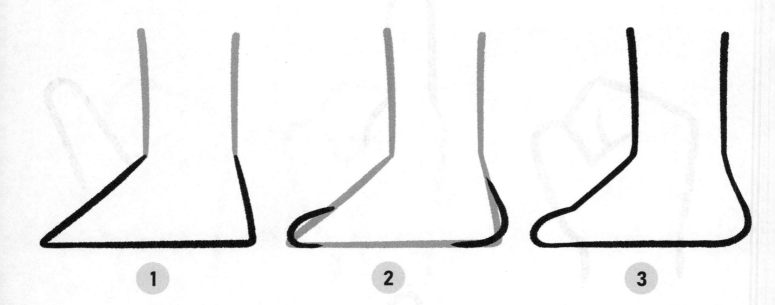

1   **2**   **3**

Trace the outline of the foot

Draw the foot

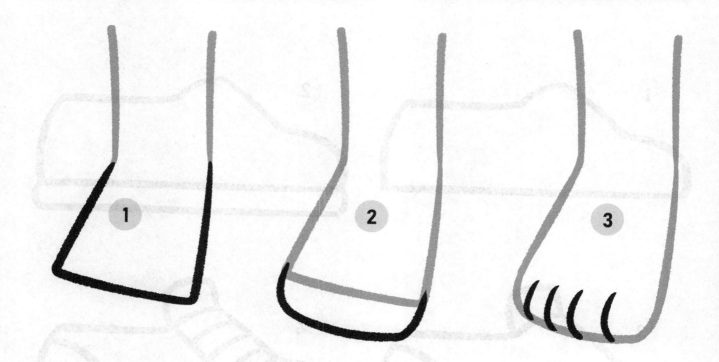

Trace the outline of the foot

Draw the foot

Profile footwear

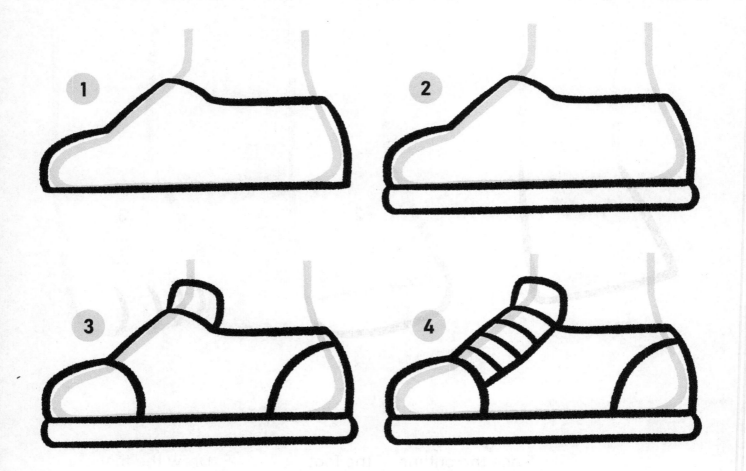

Trace the outline of the footwear

Draw the footwear

90

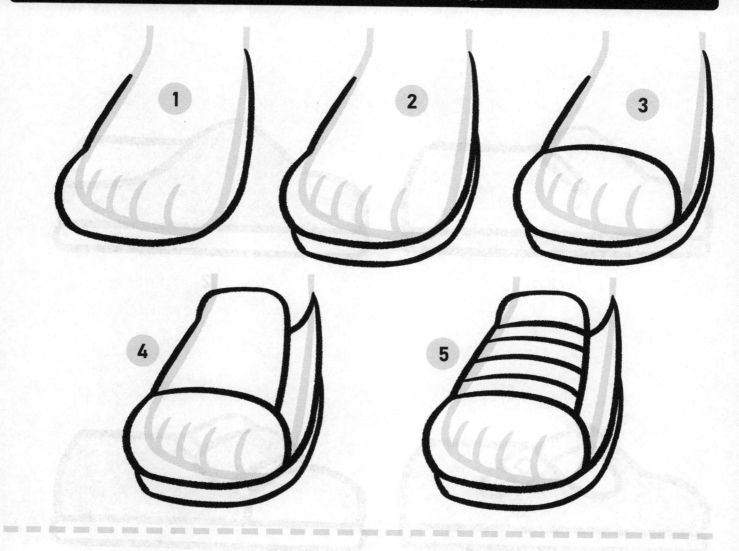

Trace the outline of the footwear

Draw the footwear

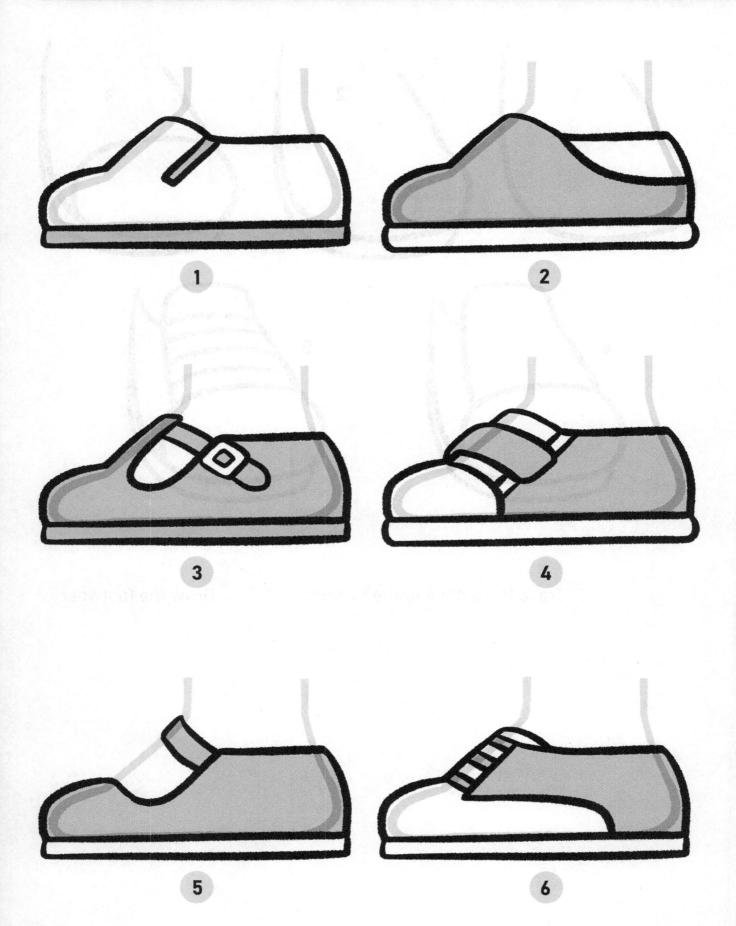

1

2

3

4

5

6

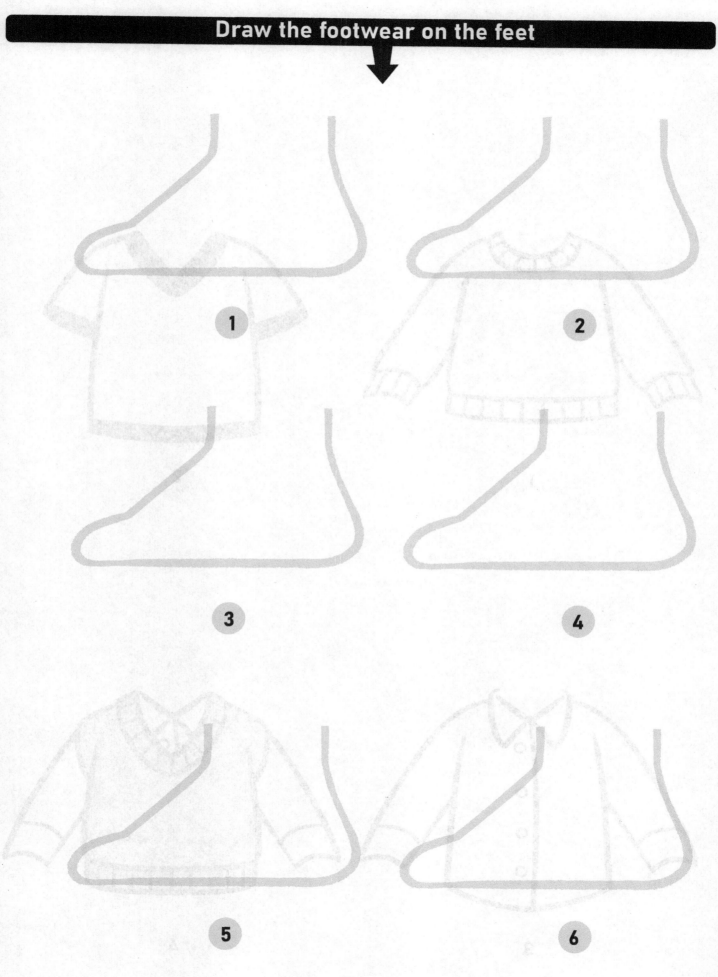

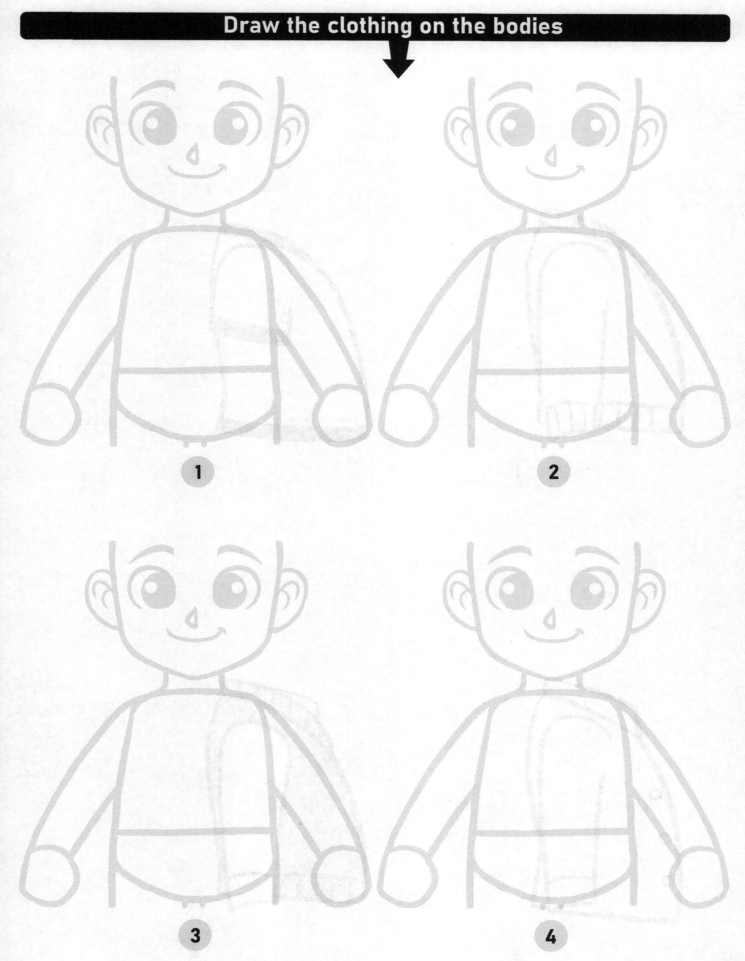

1

2

3

4

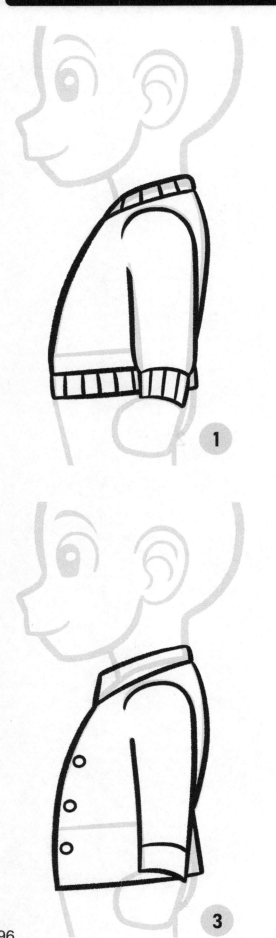

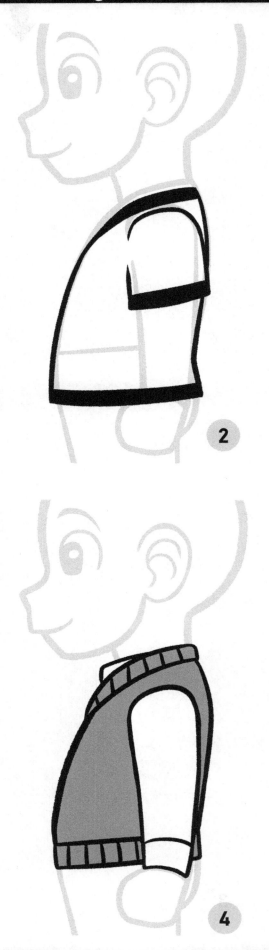

1

2

3

4

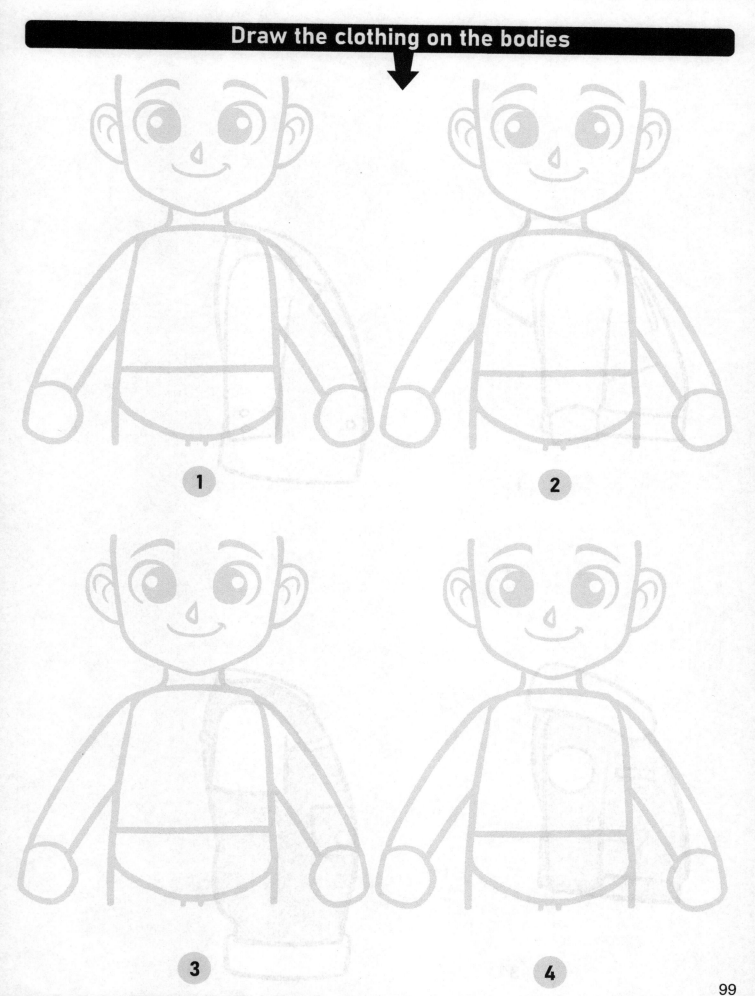

1

2

3

4

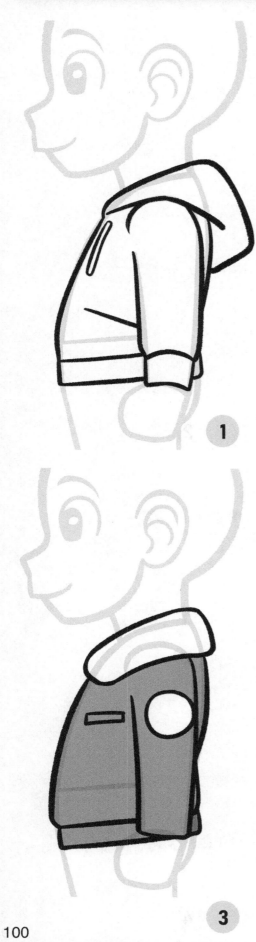

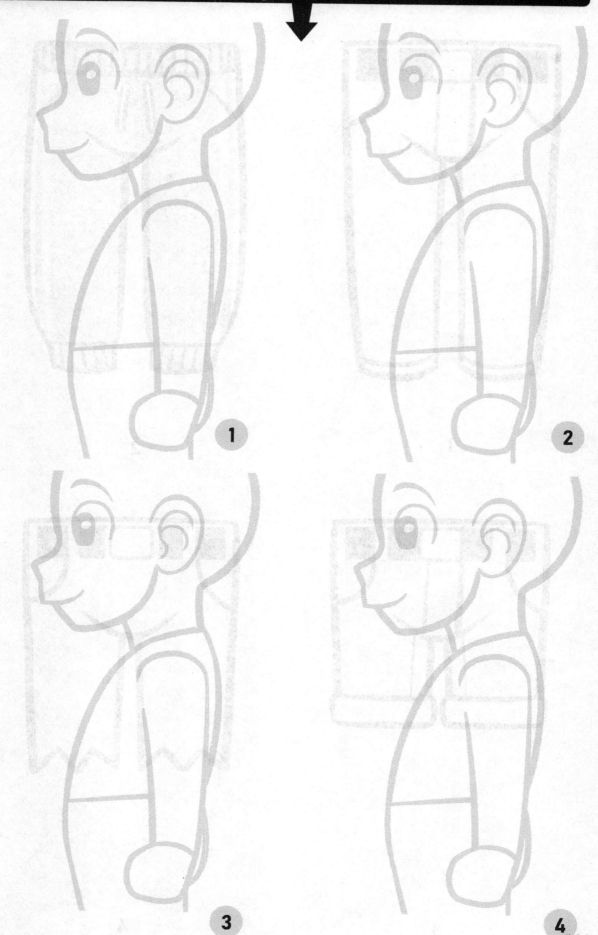

1

2

3

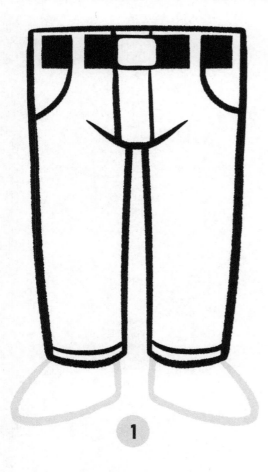

1

2

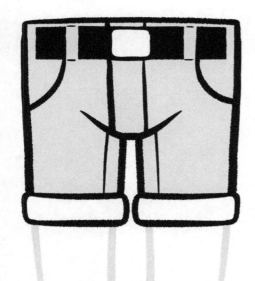

3

4

1

2

3

4

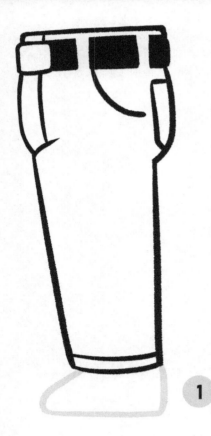

1

2

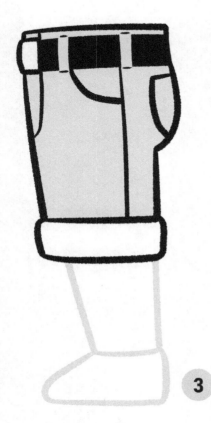

3

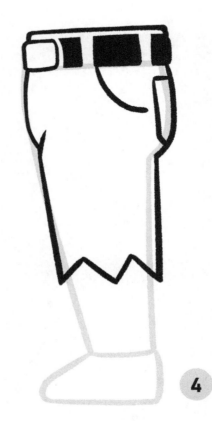

4

Skirts

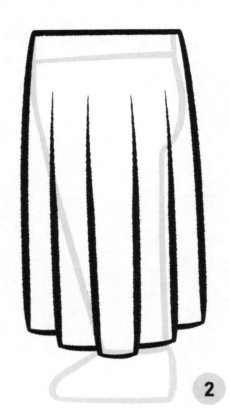

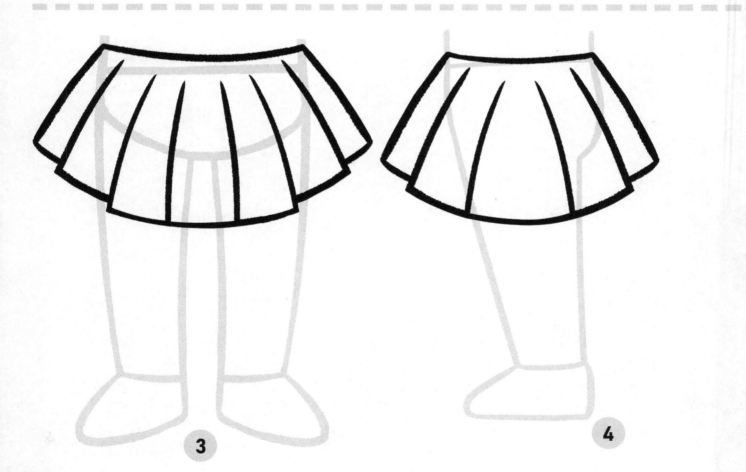

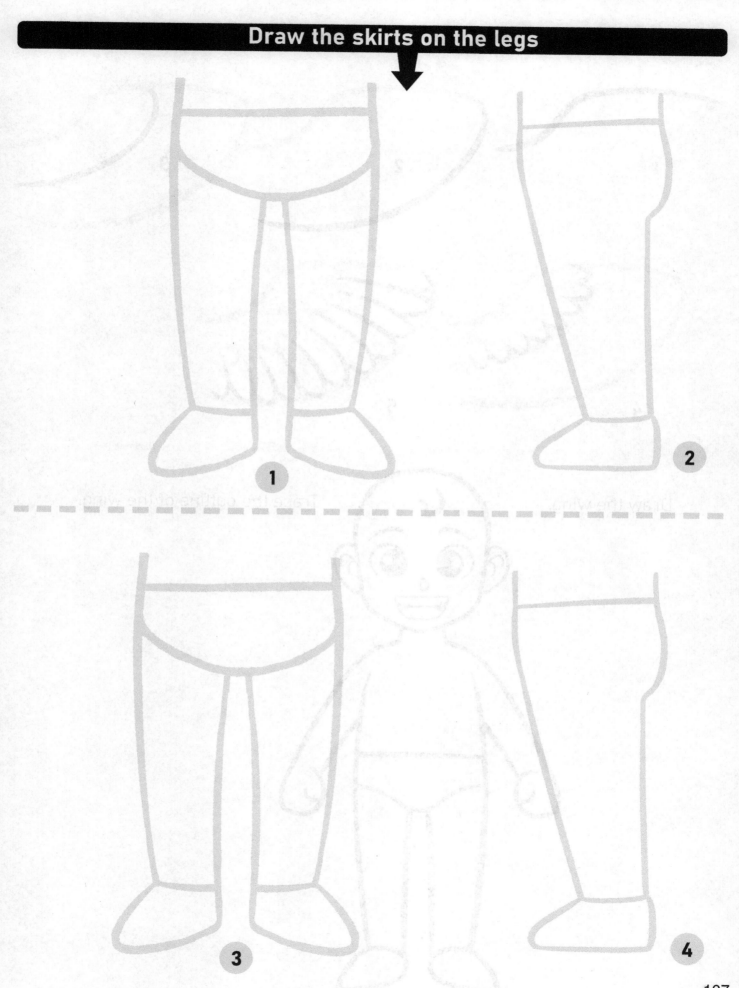

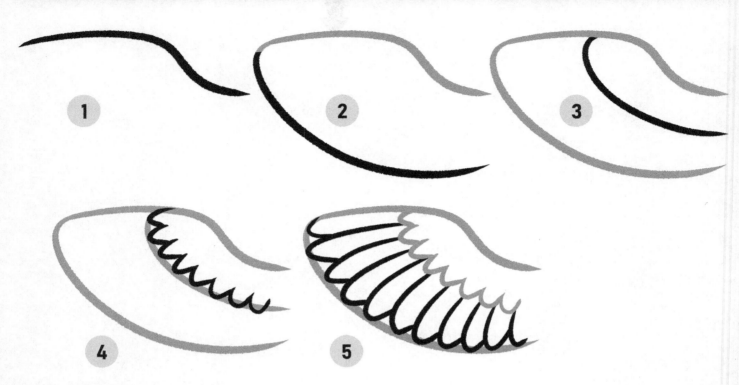

1
2
3
4
5

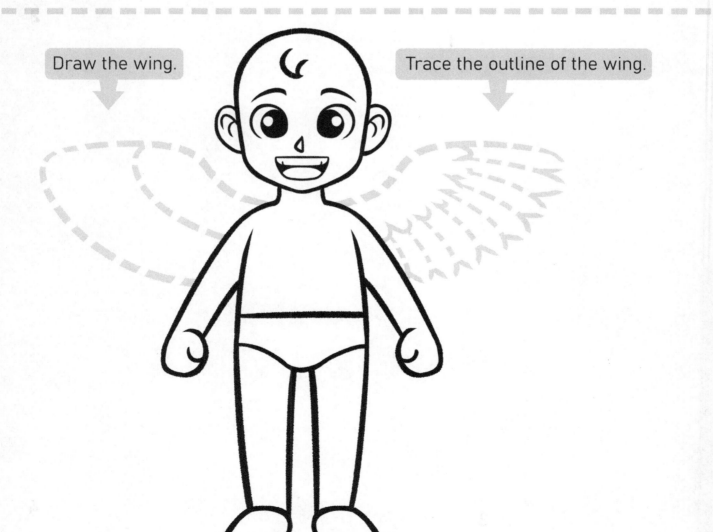

Draw the wing.

Trace the outline of the wing.

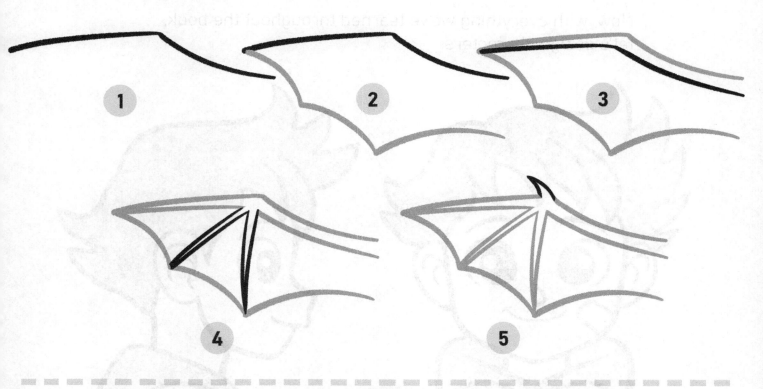

1

2

3

4

5

Draw the wing.

Trace the outline of the wing.

Character design

Now, with everything we've learned throughout the book, let's design characters.

Draw the character design

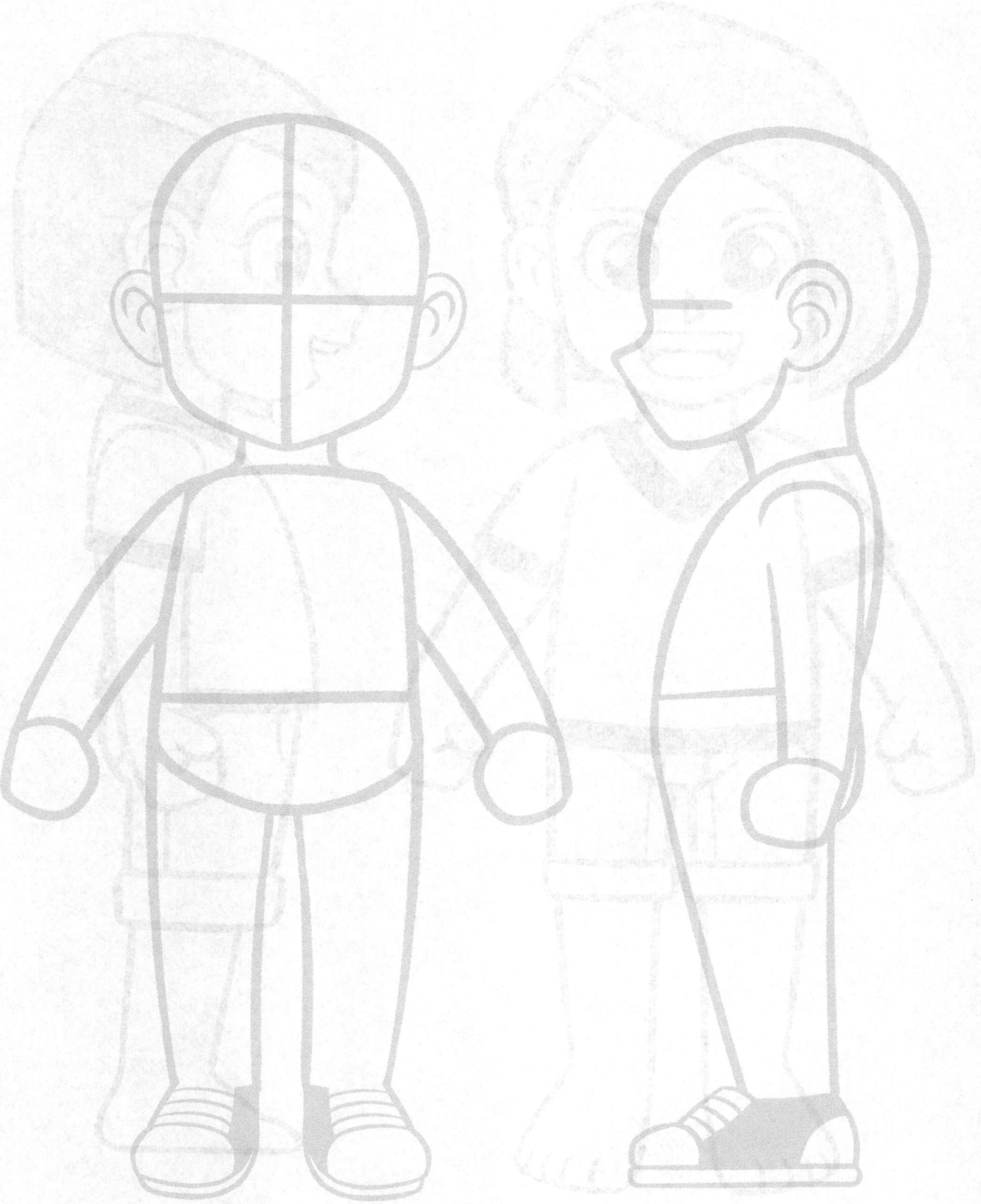

Draw the character design

NEVER STOP DRAWING AND EXPLORING YOUR CREATIVITY!

Made in the USA
Las Vegas, NV
29 November 2024

12930158R00070